PRICE STERN SLOAN

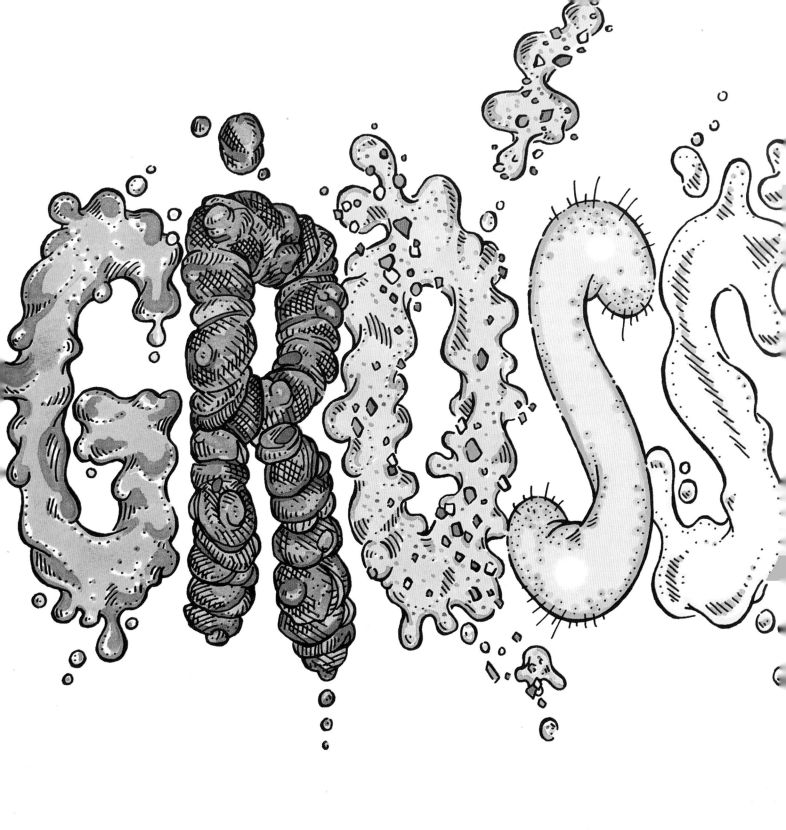

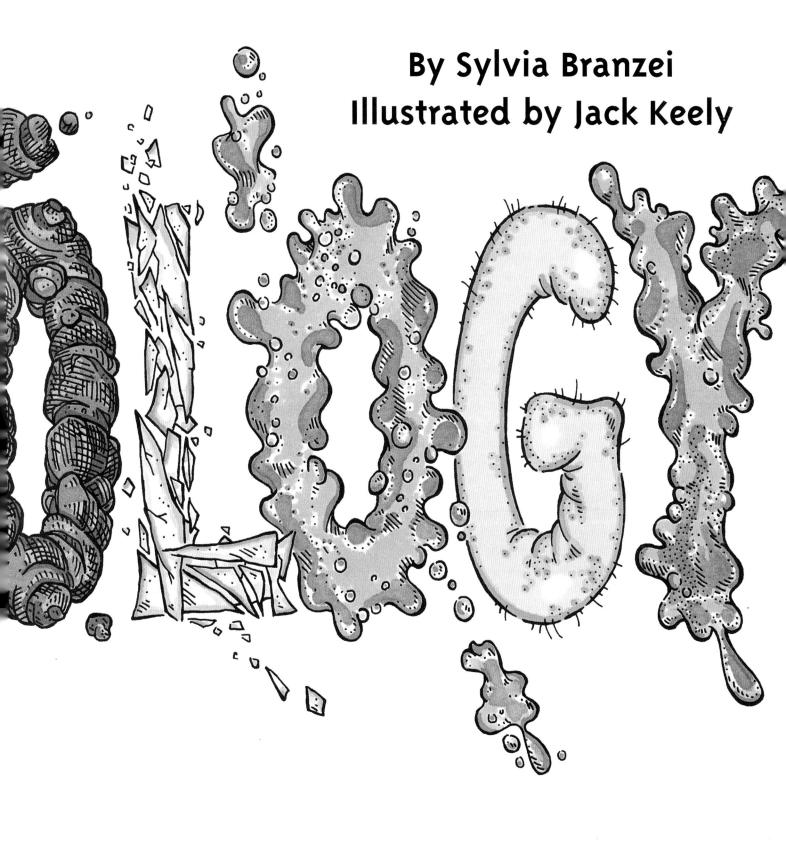

By Sylvia Branzei

Illustrated by Jack Keely

ACKNOWLEDGMENTS

This book is dedicated to all future Grossologists
and to Byron, Ian, and Alison for their gross help.—S.B.

For Darline.—J.K.

Book design by Skolos/Wedell

Special thanks to Chris St. Cyr, design wizard extraordinaire

And Now a Message from Our Corporate Lawyer:

Crosstents

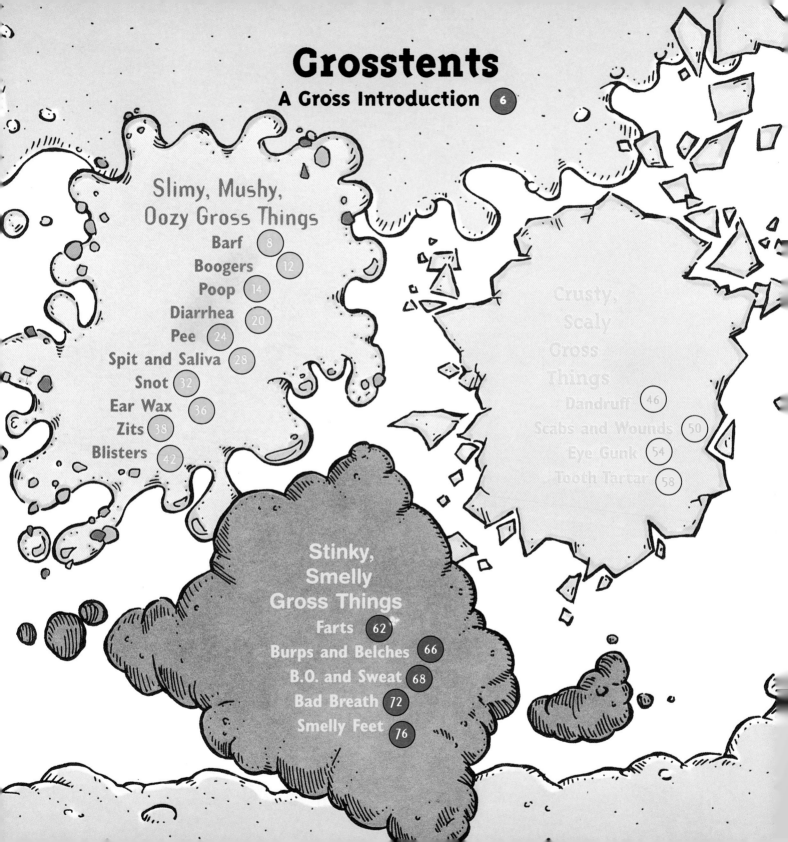

A Gross Introduction 6

A Gross Introduction

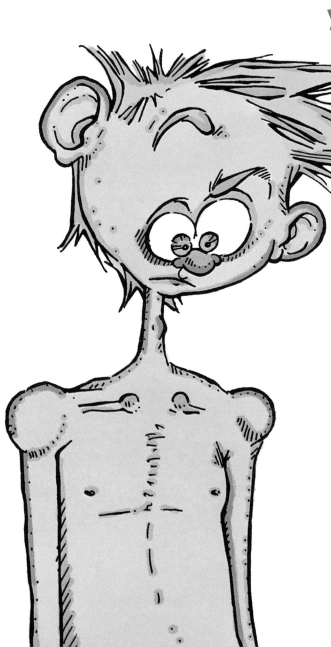

Sometimes it's stinky. Sometimes it's crusty. And sometimes it's slimy. **But hey, it's your body.** Most of the time you don't find your own smells and scabs and oozes too disgusting. It is usually the stuff on someone else's body that's really gross. But the reasons for the ickiness are identical whether it is you, your uncle, your teacher, or the kid down the street. In reading this book you will become a grossologist, and as a beginning grossologist, you will find out lots and lots of sickening things about people.

If you love to wallow in the grosser side of life, you may want to become a more experienced grossologist. It isn't very difficult—you just need a strong stomach. Read about all the things that make most people turn up their noses in disgust—like the fact that over your lifetime, you will make enough saliva to fill several large swimming pools. That's 25,000 quarts!

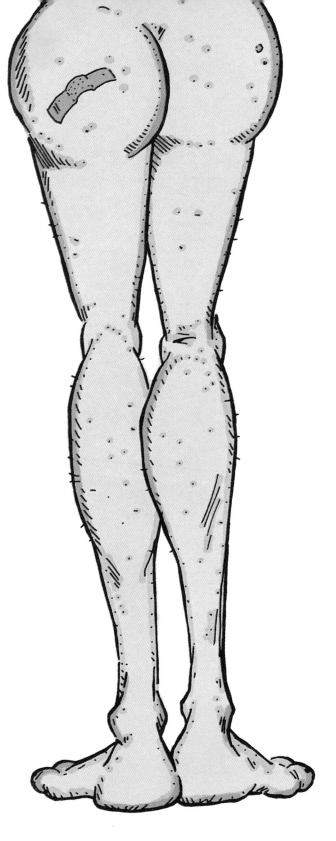

During the Middle Ages, picking your nose in public was acceptable. However, a Miss Manners of the period might have told you, "If some nose garbage falls to the ground, quickly grind it under your foot." Make sure you spread this type of disgusting information so others can enjoy and appreciate the grosser side of life as well! Also, it is very interesting to watch how other people react. So tell your mother, brother, dad, sister, grandparents, aunties, uncles, neighbors, cousins, friends, teachers, bus drivers, and anyone else who will listen about the ickiness. But keep in mind—the gross-out factor is different for everyone. For a topic that makes you want to upchuck your cookies, your cousin might say, "that's nice," and take another bite of her sandwich.

Slimy,
Mushy,
Oozy
Gross
Things

Here comes dinner! Your mouth begins to water; your stomach muscles clamp; you take a deep breath as you race toward the bathroom; you stand above the porcelain master; your throat and mouth open. Rrrrraaaaaaalllllllllffffffff. Dinner is revisiting!

After a really heavy bout of upchucking, some people say they puked their guts out. This claim just isn't true. Your guts stay right where they are; only the stuff in the gut's holding tank is expelled. If you conducted a barf analysis for the contents of puke before flushing or cleaning it up, you would find out a lot about throwing up. Of course, throw-up contains anything not digested from your last meal. Most often, you notice the hard-to-digest, tough stuff like fruits and vegetables. But that's not all there is to barf. There's the clear, slimy, liquid stuff. The slime is stomach, or gastric, mucus (MEW cuss) mixed with a dab of slippery saliva. Glands dump mucus into your stomach to protect the walls from being eaten away by acids. Before you upchuck, the walls of your stomach are irritated, so even more mucus oozes than usual. The acids

Gross! A close-up of bacteria in your intestine. © David M. Phillips that eat up the food in your stomach are also part of the barf mixture. The belly acid called hydrochloric acid is so strong that it can eat up stainless steel razor blades. The acid is diluted by the mucus and food. Other interesting features of puke are enzymes (EN zimes) that eat up butter fat, meats, and starches. Stomach juices corrode and destroy, so when they are forced into your throat, they continue to do their job. That is why your throat may feel sore after you throw up. And that's it for the stomach contents lying on the bathroom floor!

But what about the lovely green color of barf? Yes, the lovely green is not stomach contents at all. It's bile that comes from your little gut tube, or small intestine. Puking usually collects stuff from the beginning of your intestine as well as your stomach. The beginning of the intestine mostly holds completely ground-up food called chyme (KIME) and bile. Bile is made from salts, cholesterol like the kind you get from fatty food, and bilirubin, a pigment that makes throw-up green and your poop brown. So the next time you barf, you can say, "Wow, I just ejected mucus, saliva, hydrochloric acid, enzymes, chyme, bile, and dinner!"

If you ask most people, "What is the most disgusting thing your body does?" they will say, "vomit." Try taking a survey of the people you know, such as your classmates, your family, and grocery-store cashiers. But be prepared to stomach the intimate sharing of each person's most memorable vomit moments. For some reason, people remember and enjoy telling puke stories.

Even most of the words for throwing up sound gross: vomit, barf, puke, upchuck. Yet puking is pretty important for your body. It gets rid of stuff that your body thinks could be dangerous to you. In fact, throwing up is so important that there is part of the brain called the vomit center that causes this uncontrollable act. Once the vomit center goes into action, you cannot help but let loose. Four different things can excite the vomit center to bring on barf.

The most common cause of vomiting is anything that bothers the lining of the stomach. Eating or drinking too much, poisonous substances, germs like bacteria or viruses, and body infections can all cause the stomach to become irritable. And when the stomach gets mad, watch out! Your whole body gets sick.

Parts in your ear and brain are responsible for balance. If the brain can't understand the information sent to it from the ear canals, it gets confused. The brain says, "This does not compute. Something is very wrong. I must do something." The something your brain does is to alert the vomit center. That's why sailing, boating, driving, and amusement-park rides are vomit makers for some people.

Women often puke when they are first pregnant. "Oh joy! I'm going to have a baby! Rrrrrrooooaaaaallllllfffff!" Chemicals called hormones (HOR moans) are actually thought to be the reason, not great joy. A woman's body changes very quickly when she becomes pregnant. These changes upset the body's balance and cause an upset stomach.

Projectile barfs happen when a person pukes a stream that shoots **across great distances,** often hitting the ceiling or reaching across the room. A projectile barf occurs when the throat closes to make a small opening for the contents to spit through. The barf comes out the same way the water does when you put your thumb over the end of a water hose. Projectile vomiting is most common in young children.

Never, never, never try to make yourself barf. It's dumb and dangerous. You should just go to school and take the test or do whatever else it is you are trying to get out of. Making yourself puke all the time can destroy your stomach, throat, mouth, and teeth.

Maybe just reading this section has made you queasy. Icky smells, unpleasant sights, putrid thoughts, and getting nervous can make you want to throw up. And sometimes you do. Scientists are not sure why the brain reacts by vomiting. Maybe it just wants to get your mind off whatever it is that's bothering you. It's not too pleasant, but it sure works.

There's not much you can do to stop puking. If you hold your mouth closed, it will probably come out of your nose. The best thing to do is just let it happen. Because barf removes liquid from your body, you should replace the lost liquid by sipping on water, tea, apple juice, or bouillon. If you keep vomiting for more than a couple of days or if you throw up blood, you should see a doctor.

Boogers

Seventy out of a hundred people admit to picking them. And about three people out of those seventy admit to eating them. Boogers! The number may even be higher. Try taking a survey of the people you know.

Boogers can be slippery or crusty. They can be yellow, green, or brown. They are always clumpy. Boogers are actually nose garbage. Each day, you suck in a small roomful of air. If the air were only gas, you would not even make boogers. But the air is filled with dust, smoke, grit, bacteria, tiny fungi, pollen, soot, little metal pieces, ash, fuzz, sand, and even itty bitty meteorites. One job of the nose is to clean the stuff out.

Rough bristles, or nose hairs, are the first air cleaners. These hairs are also called **vibrissae (veye BRIS ee)**, which is the same word for cat whiskers. Take a look at your vibrissae. Better yet, look at the nose hairs of your father, uncle, or grandfather. Grown men sprout lots of nose hairs. Vibrissae working alone would be like blowing air through a broom. Some junk would get stuck. If you dipped the broom

bristles into oil or water, imagine how much better it would trap gunk. That is exactly what happens in your nose. A sticky liquid, called mucus (MEW cuss), or snot, coats the skin and the hairs in your nose. Bits of dirt and other stuff get trapped in your nose hairs, and then they are surrounded by nose mucus. The sticky trapped stuff clumps together little by little until a big lump is formed—a real booger. If the booger hangs around, the moisture evaporates as you breathe in more dry air and you make a dry booger. If your nose has lots of mucus or if the air is very humid (has lots of water in it), the booger may stay nice and moist. The booger sticks around until you blow it out, breathe it in, or pick it.

So boogers are polluted nose mucus. Besides being very antisocial, booger eating is not a good idea because you munch on a lot of icky stuff. Actually, picking your nose isn't too clean either. If you pick your nose really hard, it will bleed. Not fun.

70 out of 100

Poop

Poop Poop Poop Poop Poop

Do you know about Thomas Crapper? He was an Englishman who during the 1800s invented the shut-off for clean water entering the toilet tank. The word "crap" comes from Crapper. Now here's the real crap on poop. Or maybe it's the real poop on crap.

Billions of dollars are spent every year on paper to wipe it away, water to flush it away, facilities to leave it in, and treatment plants to clean it up. And the money will keep flowing because we keep making it, and we always will. Poop, caca, doo-doo, dookie, poo, number two, and **feces (FEE sees)** are all names for this never-ending stream of solid waste.

Poop Poop Poop Poop Poop Poop Poop

Today you will take a poop (or maybe tomorrow if you take a poop every other day). "Take a poop" is a rather silly phrase because you really don't take anything. You actually leave it behind. The putty-like waste you deposit contains undigested food materials from the previous day, water, salts, skin cells, little living creatures called bacteria, bacteria wastes, and coloring (or pigment).

Plant fibers in vegetables will end up in the toilet. Your body takes out the nutrients from the vegetables when the food passes through your gut tube, the small intestine. The stuff your body can't use pushes on to the large intestine, another wider tube, then out of your body. Maybe you have noticed that corn kernels are not digested by your body. Rabbits also do not digest plant material well, but plants are their only food source. So to have a well-balanced diet, rabbits eat some of their dookie: bunny yummies.

In France during the late 1600s, it was considered a great honor to speak with King Louis XIV while he relieved himself on his not-so-kingly throne.

Bacteria make up about half of the material in poo. Billions of these tiny

creatures live in the part of your intestine called the colon. They gobble up bits of remaining food. In doing so, they create gases and the chemicals indole (IN dohl) and skatole (SCAT ohl). Indole and skatole help to create the familiar dookie smell that attracts flies and curious dogs. The gases created by bacteria build up and are released as farts. Farting and pooping often go together. As the undigested stuff passes through the colon, the pre-caca clumps together. The globs of poop material are separated by space that can fill with gas. If it doesn't escape ahead of time, the gas exits with the poop. So you can toot while you poop.

The Peristalsis Pinch

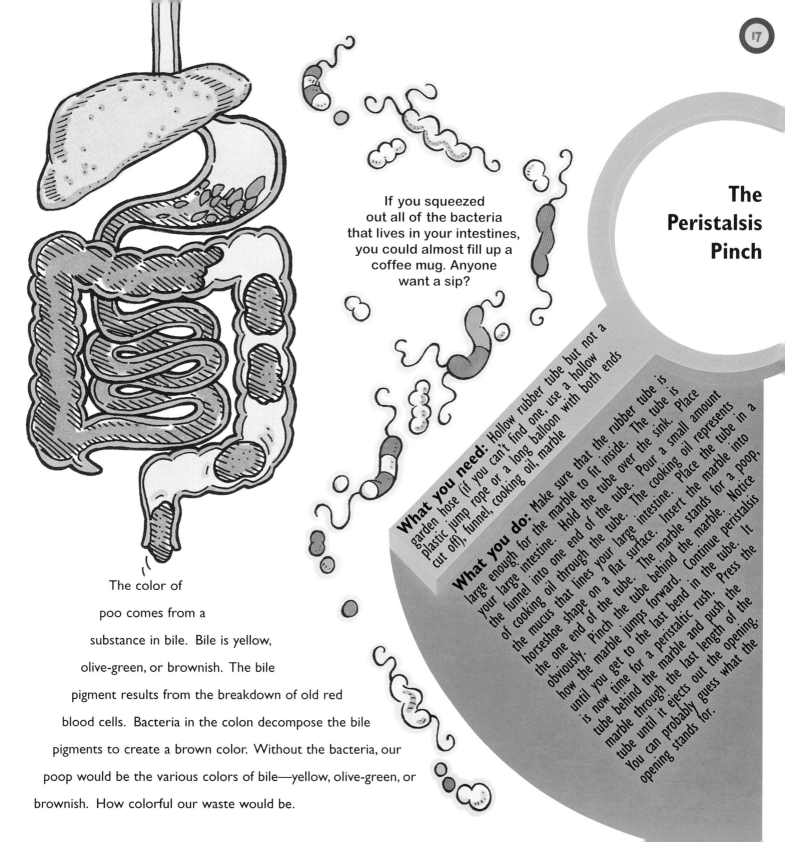

If you squeezed out all of the bacteria that lives in your intestines, you could almost fill up a coffee mug. Anyone want a sip?

The color of poo comes from a substance in bile. Bile is yellow, olive-green, or brownish. The bile pigment results from the breakdown of old red blood cells. Bacteria in the colon decompose the bile pigments to create a brown color. Without the bacteria, our poop would be the various colors of bile—yellow, olive-green, or brownish. How colorful our waste would be.

What you need: Hollow rubber tube but not a garden hose (if you can't find one, use a hollow plastic jump rope or a long balloon with both ends cut off), funnel, cooking oil, marble

What you do: Make sure that the rubber tube is large enough for the marble to fit inside. The tube is your large intestine. Hold the tube over the sink. Place the funnel into one end of the tube. Pour a small amount of cooking oil through the tube. The cooking oil represents the mucus that lines your large intestine. Place the tube in a horseshoe shape on a flat surface. Insert the marble into the one end of the tube. The marble stands for a poop, obviously. Pinch the tube behind the marble. Notice how the marble jumps forward. Continue peristalsis until you get to the last bend in the tube. It is now time for a peristaltic rush. Press the tube behind the marble and push the marble through the last length of the tube until it ejects out the opening. You can probably guess what the opening stands for.

Your poop factory is in your five-foot large intestine. The large intestine is a horseshoe-shaped, puckered tube resting below your waist. It connects on the right end to your small intestine, wraps across your waist, goes down the left side, then curls to end in the center at your anus (AY nus), or butthole. Your doo-doo delivery service is the rectum (RECK tum) and the anus. The rectum is the last eight inches of your five-foot large intestine, and it ends at the anus exit door.

You can think of your intestine as a railroad track and your poops as freight cars resting unattached to one another on the track. Every day a new car comes along and bumps the last car off of the end. Sometimes the new car arrives with a force great enough to bump off several cars. The force that creates the movement for the freight cars in your bowel, or intestine, comes from muscles. Muscles in your large intestine pinch the waste along bit by bit. This type of movement is called peristalsis (pear a STAL sis). As the liquid poop is squeezed along, water seeps through the walls of the intestine. Semisolid waste clumps together to form individual poops. When poop fills the rectum, messages sent to your brain tell you it's time to go. If you are riding in a car, your brain informs the anus exit that it had better stay shut. If you weren't taught this butthole control, you would just release your load then and there. Actually, if you hadn't mastered this technique, you would probably still wear diapers. At the right time and place, preferably on the toilet, you have a peristaltic rush. A peristaltic rush is the scientific way to say "take a dump." The muscles in your rectum shorten, increasing the pressure inside. You push with your stomach muscles. Your anus opens, and poo is ejected. Splash! Ahhhh! Relief.

Poop Power

For a long time, Chinese farmers have tapped into the power of poop. They dump pig doo-doo and other animal waste into a large holding area. The bacteria in dookie keep on doing their stuff in the dung pile, creating methane, or natural gas. A pipe inserted into the fecal dump brings the natural gas into the household for cooking. Just think, they cook pork by using the power of pork poop.

NATURAL GAS

Diarrhea

DIARRHEA! C'EST BELLE!

Say the word "diarrhea" out loud. Sounds beautiful, doesn't it? At least that's what some people thought in a study conducted on words. Researchers read a list of different English words to people who did not speak English. The non-English speakers chose words that they thought sounded pretty. Diarrhea was one word that most of the people chose. Had they known what it meant, they might not have been so impressed by the sound.

The Greek word "diarrhein," which means "to flow through," describes diarrhea very well. If you read the section on poop, you are familiar with peristalsis and peristaltic rush. Diarrhea is peristalsis and peristaltic rush gone cuckoo. Basically diarrhea happens when you poop a lot more than normal. Also, the

Then there is the diarrhea song. Don't forget to sing the diarrhea song as you trot to the pot. It won't make the runs go away, but it will add some fun to your poop-run-amok experience. If you don't know the song, reading the words will help you to figure out the tune.

Wake up in the morning.
Put your feet on the floor.
Do the 50-yard dash to the bathroom door.
Diarrhea, diarrhea!

When you're sliding into first
And you feel something burst,
Diarrhea, diarrhea!

When you're sliding into third
And you lay a juicy turd,
Diarrhea, diarrhea!

When you're sliding into home
And you feel something foam,
Diarrhea, diarrhea!

dookie fits the shape of its container, which is a way to say that it is liquidy or runny. The nickname "the runs" explains both the look of the feces and the fact that you are constantly trotting to the toilet.

When your guts, the small or large intestine, become irritated, you get diarrhea. "I'm feeling so perturbed that I'll just push this stuff on through and get it over with," is what an irritated gut tube does. The muscles in the intestine pinch more often to move the mush along so fast that water is not removed. And the agitated intestine adds to the problem further by weeping fluids: "I'm so mad I'm going to cry." The result is large amounts of watery poop.

The most common reason for developing diarrhea is the intestinal flu. Teeny, tiny, simple creatures called viruses invade the bowels and hang out. As long as the viruses are present, the bowels weep and pinch and squirt. This disease usually lasts for several days, and the sufferer becomes very familiar with the inside of the bathroom during this time. Over a hundred different diseases can cause diarrhea. Stress, food allergies, food poisons, milk intolerance, and some medicines also create diarrhea. It's amazing that we don't have the runs all of the time instead of just one or two days a year.

Montezuma's revenge, turkey trot, Hong Kong dog, Aztec two-step, Trotskys, and Delhi belly: what could all of these names have in common? They are all types of traveler's diarrhea. Over 200 million Americans travel to another country every year, and about 50 million of them get diarrhea. Scientists have traveled all over the world studying traveler's diarrhea. Some researchers convince a group of travelers to leave behind a poop sample before they leave, mail back feces while they are away, and then make one more deposit after they return. Other studies include scientists trailing along with the travelers, collecting and analyzing dookie samples as they happen. The grand prize from all of this research is the knowledge that traveler's diarrhea is a result of swallowing or drinking different types of bacteria, viruses, and other

The Kayap tribe from the Amazon are such experimental eaters that their language contains about 100 different words for diarrhea.

creatures. Although travelers get the disease, the local people do not. People are used to the types of microcreatures in their area, so they are not affected by them. *Does that mean I should never leave my own backyard?* Actually, if you stayed home, you would never get the Aztec two-step or Trotskys. But choosing foods carefully and drinking bottled water if you leave the country sounds a lot more fun.

Chances are very high that you will get some type of the runs in the next year, even if you do stay home. The best treatment for diarrhea is time. It should go away within a couple of days. Because you lose liquid during your poop attack, you should drink lots of fluids that contain sugar and salts. Drinks used for quenching thirst after heavy exercise are best. There are also some medicines that you can buy to soak up the water or slow down peristalsis.

Pee

Some South American natives drink it as a refreshment: "yummy." There are people all over the world who drink it because they believe it is healthy: "Drink it. It's good for you." It has also been used for a mouthwash by some Native American tribes: "Gargle, gargle." It was even good for tanning leather used in shoes and clothing: "Let's wear it." And many, many years ago, it served as a cleaning agent for people: "Use it for all-purpose cleaning."

Hold on. I thought this section was on pee. Yep, pee, or urine. That's what some people drink (*Gag*) and swish (*Ack*) and swipe (*Gross*). Actually, pee isn't as disgusting as it seems. About 96 percent of urine is extra water that your body didn't need. The rest is salts, urea (yur EE a), vitamins your body didn't use, pigments, and other stuff that your body didn't need.

Fresh urine is cleaner than poop, spit, or the skin on your face because healthy pee is not home to bacteria. Only if you let it sit in the toilet for a while will the bacteria in the air find the pee and move in. The urea in old pee breaks down to form ammonia and carbon dioxide.

The ammonia gives stale pee a strong smell. Ammonia is used as a cleaning fluid in many houses, but the ammonia you buy at the store is not made from pee. The ammonia that was used by ancient people, however, was the product of stale urine.

Although they both end up in the toilet, the pee system is separate from the poop system in your body. Urine never mingles with poop in your intestines or even in your organs that deposit waste. Pee is produced in the kidneys. It travels directly to the bladder, then exits through the urethra (you REE thra), a tube that connects your bladder to your pee hole.

Every day you make and deliver four to eight cups of urine. The amount depends upon a lot of things like how hot it is, what

WOMEN

You have probably noticed a long line at the women's restroom while there is no line at the men's restroom. A group of college students conducted a study to find out why. Men average about forty-five seconds to use the toilet, while women spend about seventy-nine seconds. The extra seconds add to a long wait.

you eat, and how much you drink. You can find out for yourself how much pee you make by doing the activity. The reason that you pee more than once a day is that the bladder can't hold all eight cups. It can hold only about two cups comfortably because your tinkle storage sack just isn't big enough. An empty bladder looks like a shriveled-up balloon or a prune that is about three-and-a-half inches wide. The kidneys drip pee into your bladder. As it fills up, the bladder stretches like a water balloon. As the pee-pee balloon becomes stretched, little message centers in the bladder tell your brain, "Guess what? You had better go pee." Then the bladder loosens a ring of muscle around the hole at the base. Luckily, the bladder has another ring of muscles below the one that the bladder controls. This ring of muscles answers to the brain. Because the brain is in control of the moment you actually pee, it answers back, "Hey, don't bother me. I'm busy." This delaying can go on for a little while longer, until the bladder is all filled up. "Hey, brain, I can't wait. I've got to go NOW!" This time you'd better do something about it and quick. Controlling your bladder muscles is learned. That is why babies get potty trained.

If you eat lots of red beets, your pee will actually be colored red.

The average person passes 9,202 gallons of urine in his or her lifetime. That's enough to fill 315 bathtubs!

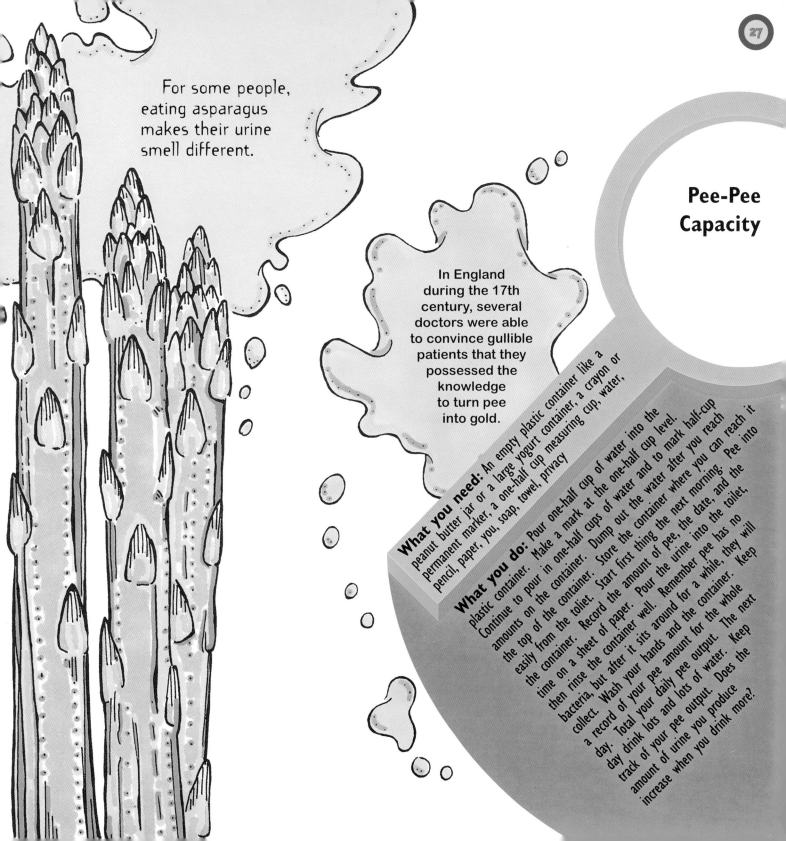

For some people, eating asparagus makes their urine smell different.

In England during the 17th century, several doctors were able to convince gullible patients that they possessed the knowledge to turn pee into gold.

Pee-Pee Capacity

What you need: An empty plastic container like a peanut butter jar or a large yogurt container, a crayon or permanent marker, a one-half cup measuring cup, water, pencil, paper, you, soap, towel, privacy

What you do: Pour one-half cup of water into the plastic container. Make a mark at the one-half cup level. Continue to pour in one-half cups of water and to mark half-cup amounts on the container. Dump out the water after you reach the top of the container. Store the container where you can reach it easily from the toilet. Start first thing the next morning. Pee into the container. Record the amount of pee, the date, and the time on a sheet of paper. Pour the urine into the toilet, then rinse the container well. Remember pee has no bacteria, but after it sits around for a while, they will collect. Wash your hands and the container. Keep a record of your pee amount for the whole day. Total your daily pee output. The next day drink lots and lots of water. Keep track of your daily pee output. Does the amount of urine you produce increase when you drink more?

Spit and Saliva

A whiff of vinegar is guaranteed to make your mouth water. Actually, mouths water just thinking about food. But some food thoughts work better than others. Maybe you know a kid who always says, "You can't make me do anything I don't want to." Find that kid and explain that you can make the kid's mouth water. Start describing delicious foods like chocolate-chip cookies fresh from the oven, cold pink lemonade, potato chips and dip. Even if the "you can't make me" kid tells you it's not working, it is. The kid can't stop it. Be careful though that this kid doesn't become angry and try to throw a mouth's contents, or spit, at you. Uck! Run away, quick.

The stuff your mouth produces is not all water. That's why it is called spit, or saliva (sah LIE vuh). OK, most of it is water—99.5 percent of it. The other little nonwater bit has a bunch of different chemicals. Saliva contains substances that destroy bacteria,

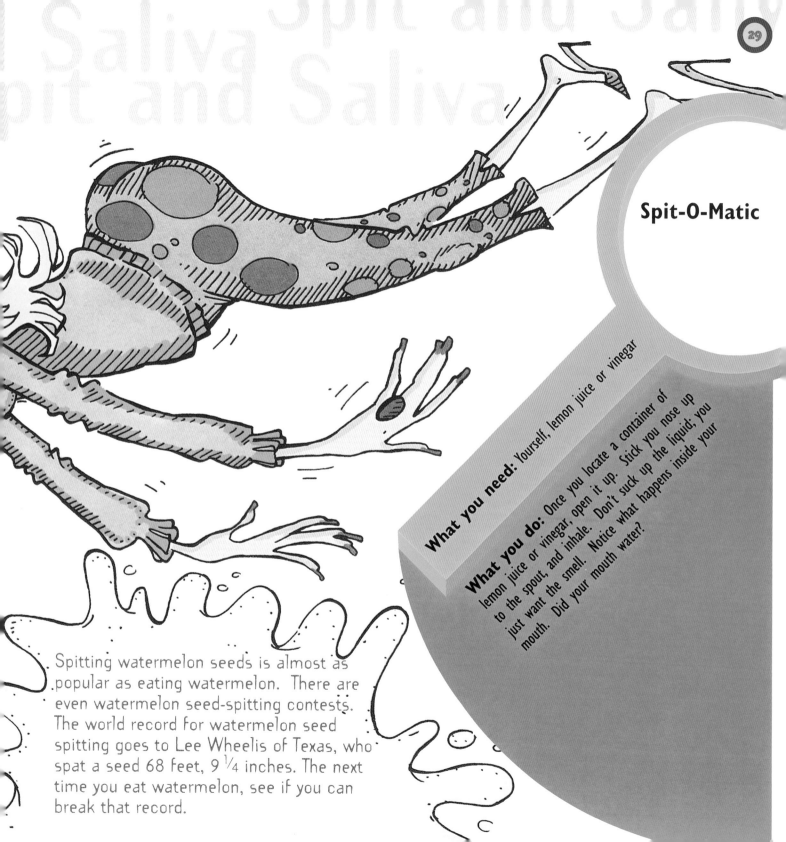

Spit-O-Matic

What you need: Yourself, lemon juice or vinegar

What you do: Once you locate a container of lemon juice or vinegar, open it up. Stick you nose up to the spout, and inhale. Don't suck up the liquid; you just want the smell. Notice what happens inside your mouth. Did your mouth water?

Spitting watermelon seeds is almost as popular as eating watermelon. There are even watermelon seed-spitting contests. The world record for watermelon seed spitting goes to Lee Wheelis of Texas, who spat a seed 68 feet, 9 ¼ inches. The next time you eat watermelon, see if you can break that record.

Saliva Magic: Turning Starch into Sugar

For the Masai people of Tanzania, Africa, spitting is considered a show of goodwill. Newborn babies are spat upon to bring the child luck, and deals are often closed only after the traders spit upon one another.

What you need: Yourself, a soda cracker (salt free works best), a little time

What to do: Put a mouth-size piece of soda cracker on your tongue. Close your mouth but don't chew. Leave the cracker there for several minutes to let the saliva do its thing. Remember, **DON'T CHEW!** After several minutes, swish the cracker in your mouth and swallow. How did the cracker taste?

salts, gases, antacids, mucus, chemicals that break down food called **enzymes (EN zimes)**, and **urine.** *Urine! There's pee in my mouth?* Yep, all people have potty mouths. A small trickle of pee enters your mouth from the places in your body that make saliva. These are called glands.

Your spit factories are located in several glands. Many tiny glands line the inside of your cheeks and ooze small amounts of saliva. Pairs of spit makers are hidden in front of each ear, under the tongue, and beneath the lower jaw. Spit travels in tubes, or ducts, from the glands to pour spit into the mouth. Think of a liter soda bottle. That's about how much saliva enters your mouth every day. Now think of 190 liter soda bottles. That's how much saliva a hay-eating cow produces daily!

Spit is **great** stuff. It gets food wet so it's easy to swallow. It **kills bacteria** in the mouth that can cause cavities. It's a **natural mouthwash.** And it **turns starch into sugar.** Now that's a real trick. The enzymes in saliva break apart long starch molecules and turn them into short sugar molecules. Life is sweet with saliva around.

Spit Test

What you need: Two crackers, yourself, tincture of iodine (you can buy it at the drugstore in the first aid section), two glass bowls or dishes or small cups

What you do: Crunch up a cracker into one of the glass containers. Add several drops of iodine. If the iodine turns black or dark blue, there is starch in the food. What color is the iodine? Chew up the other cracker. **DO NOT EAT** the cracker with iodine on it! Iodine is poisonous; it tastes really awful, and you will mess up the experiment. Keep chewing until the cracker is all mushy. **DON'T SWALLOW.** Spit out the chewed up cracker onto the clean glass container. Add several drops of iodine. What color is the iodine?

Camels and llamas actually spit when they are angry. The target of their spit attack is the eye.

Snot

Snot is one part of your daily diet that you never think about. *Snot?* **Yep, you swallow about a quart of it each day.** Just think: you swallow more snot than you drink milk. It's not that you pour a big glass of snot and say, "Oh, I need my daily glass of snot." It travels from your nose area to the back of your throat, and you just swallow it into your stomach.

Snot is a slippery liquid called nose mucus (MEW cuss) mixed with a special bacteria-killing chemical. Snot is a thick liquid clear as glass. *Clear as glass? How about yellowish green?* When you blow your nose, the snot may not be clear because it is mixed with gunk from the air. If you have a cold, the yellow or green color in your snot is actually bacteria and bacterial waste.

Snot keeps junk from reaching your lungs. Snot is so important that your nose makes a new batch every twenty minutes. To keep the old stuff from just dripping out your nostrils, your nose is filled with hairs. If you read about boogers, you already know about these. Some of the hairs are big

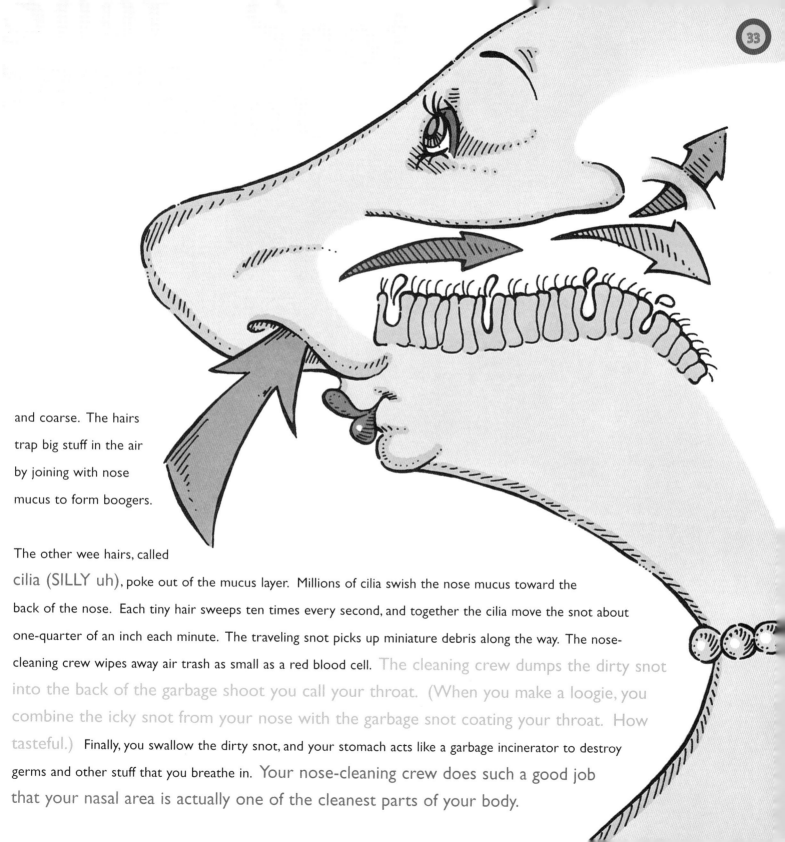

and coarse. The hairs trap big stuff in the air by joining with nose mucus to form boogers.

The other wee hairs, called cilia (SILLY uh), poke out of the mucus layer. Millions of cilia swish the nose mucus toward the back of the nose. Each tiny hair sweeps ten times every second, and together the cilia move the snot about one-quarter of an inch each minute. The traveling snot picks up miniature debris along the way. The nose-cleaning crew wipes away air trash as small as a red blood cell. The cleaning crew dumps the dirty snot into the back of the garbage shoot you call your throat. (When you make a loogie, you combine the icky snot from your nose with the garbage snot coating your throat. How tasteful.) Finally, you swallow the dirty snot, and your stomach acts like a garbage incinerator to destroy germs and other stuff that you breathe in. Your nose-cleaning crew does such a good job that your nasal area is actually one of the cleanest parts of your body.

In some Eskimo tribes, it is customary for mothers to suck the snot from their baby's noses and spit it upon the ground.

You notice the cilia's hard work of keeping snot flowing only when they don't work at all. When you go from a warm place to a cold one, your cilia slow down or even freeze. Snot comes pouring out from the front of your nose like a faucet. Or if the air spaces inside your skull, called sinuses (SY nesses), become blocked, the mucus just sits there, fills with gunk, and becomes thick and globby. The cilia quit working; the new snot dripping into your nose doesn't get pushed along; and you get a stuffed-up nose or postnasal drip. Since your air-cleaning system is not doing its job, the snot hangs around and gets dirtier, and bacteria grow inside. Thick, blobby, yellow-green snot is the reward. Some people have runny noses much of the time because they have allergies (AL er jeez). For these people, common things like dust, pollen, or animals cause their bodies to give off a chemical that orders the nose, "Make more mucus and block off those sinuses with swelling." The nose follows the orders, so allergy sufferers drip lots of clear snot and sniff a lot.

It snot over yet, is it? Yep, it is.

Ear Wax

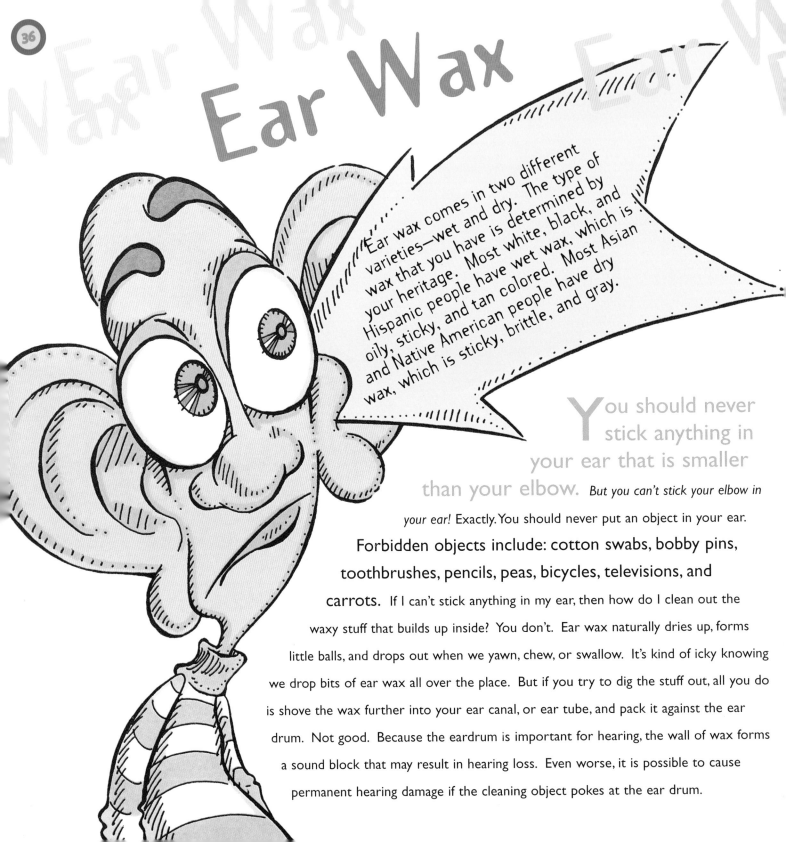

Ear wax comes in two different varieties—wet and dry. The type of wax that you have is determined by your heritage. Most white, black, and Hispanic people have wet wax, which is oily, sticky, and tan colored. Most Asian and Native American people have dry wax, which is sticky, brittle, and gray.

You should never stick anything in your ear that is smaller than your elbow. *But you can't stick your elbow in your ear!* Exactly. You should never put an object in your ear. Forbidden objects include: cotton swabs, bobby pins, toothbrushes, pencils, peas, bicycles, televisions, and carrots. If I can't stick anything in my ear, then how do I clean out the waxy stuff that builds up inside? You don't. Ear wax naturally dries up, forms little balls, and drops out when we yawn, chew, or swallow. It's kind of icky knowing we drop bits of ear wax all over the place. But if you try to dig the stuff out, all you do is shove the wax further into your ear canal, or ear tube, and pack it against the ear drum. Not good. Because the eardrum is important for hearing, the wall of wax forms a sound block that may result in hearing loss. Even worse, it is possible to cause permanent hearing damage if the cleaning object pokes at the ear drum.

The ear has three parts: the outer, middle, and inner ear. The outer ear is the part you can observe by using your eyes or a special ear wax checker that you can make using a flashlight and a plastic cone. The outer ear is also where ear wax, or cerumen (suh ROO men), is made. Inside the ear canal are about two thousand special sweat glands. These glands don't make sweat; they make wax. Ear wax coats the inside of the ear canal to trap any nasty stuff like dirt, dust, and bugs that get into your ear. People who live in areas with a lot of junk in the air, such as New York City, make more ear wax. Once something is stuck in your ear wax, the wax becomes less sticky, clumps, and falls out. To search for waxy build-up, take a look into the ear of someone you love.

The Great Wax Detector

What you need: A small flashlight or a penlight that works, a plastic bottle, scissors, paint and a brush or permanent marker, tape, a willing volunteer.

What you do: Remove the cap of the plastic bottle. Use the scissors to cut off the top part of the bottle, so that you end up with something that looks like a funnel. Trim the top of the bottle until it fits snugly onto the end of the flashlight. Coat the inside of the bottle top with dark paint or permanent marker. Allow the paint or marker to dry. Tape the top of the bottle to the end of the flashlight. Find a willing volunteer. To look into the right ear, have your volunteer straighten the ear canal by pinching the back of the ear flap, then pulling it upward and toward the back of the head. Place your ear wax detector up to the opening of the ear canal. Turn on the flashlight. Conduct your ear wax search. Say things like "How many years have you had a dime stuck in your ear?"

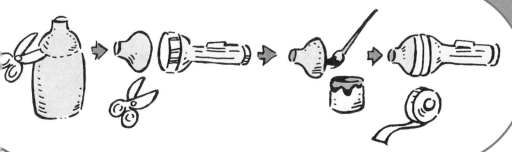

Zits

Quick! Name the largest organ of the human body. Did you say the heart? The stomach? The intestine? **It is actually the skin.** Get your hands on a magnifying glass, and look at your skin. The skin surface has hairs and little holes, or pores. Often hairs poke out from the pores, but some pores do not have hair companions. You may also see little flakes. These flakes are dead skin cells. You shed skin every day to produce a whole new layer of skin every twenty-eight days.

Gigantic germs living on your skin! © David Scharf 1986

The Ultimate Teenage Zit Control

1. Wash your face several times daily with a mild soap.
2. Apply a zit product that contains benzoyl peroxide to the zitty area. (Unless you can see actual zits, don't put this stuff on. Prezits, pretend zits, and panic nonzits are not acne.)
3. Don't put skin creams or oily make-up on your face. Use nongreasy sunscreens.
4. Stay calm. Stress increases zit flare-up.

Oily Skin Test

Also on your skin is a bunch of stuff that you can't see with a magnifying glass. Small amounts of blood cells, pus, oil, and sweat are released from your pores. A huge number of living creatures survive on your skin as well. These creatures, called bacteria, sway, roll, bounce, swim, eat, and reproduce on your skin. They are so small that a dozen could line up across one pore. On your legs about 8,000 bacteria live in each square inch. But that's nothing compared to your nose, cheek, and chin that house more than 2,000,000. Now don't go running to scrub your face. No matter how many times you wash your face, no matter how hard you scrub, you can never get rid of all the bacteria. And actually it's OK. The little critters don't hurt you.

What you need: Your face, washcloth, soap, water, rubbing alcohol, cotton swab, clock, small square of tissue paper

What you do: Use the washcloth and soap to clean your forehead. Use the cotton swab to scrub your forehead. Wait four hours. Do not touch your forehead during this time. After four hours, firmly smear the tissue across your forehead. If more than half the paper has an oil mark, your skin is oily. If a light oil smudge is on the paper, your skin is normal. If there is no oil smudge, your skin is dry.

Hey, wait! There are more bacteria! These microcritters live right under the skin surface. They burrow down because they hate oxygen and prefer to live under the always-present surface grease. Under the grease layer on your forehead are about 8,000,000 critters for each square inch. That's a larger population of bacteria in one square inch under your forehead than the entire number of people in Kentucky and Tennessee combined! Just like the creatures that live on the top of your skin, these under-the-oily-surface critters don't hurt you.

None of the skin features alone is a problem. However, a combination of dead skin cells, pores, skin oils called sebum (SEA bum), and bacteria is the recipe for zits. The medical word for zits is acne (ACK nee). Acne includes blackheads, pimples, and cysts. Cysts are large, painful blemishes. Almost all people get some acne during life. But the cruel fact is that zits, blackheads, pimples, and cysts are most common in teenagers. A teenager's body is changing so fast that the body chemicals are going wild and make huge amounts of sebum. In time, the oil glands will slow down and behave themselves.

A treatment for acne prescribed around 350 A.D. was to watch for a falling star, then wipe the pimples away with a cloth as the star fell.

All forms of acne start out the same way. Dead skin cells shed inside pores. **The dead skin cells then clump together with sebum, bacteria, and bacterial waste in the pore and form a comedo (COM ee dough).** The word "comedo" actually means "fat maggot" in Latin, because early doctors thought that these bumps were really maggots under the skin eating the sebum. Gross.

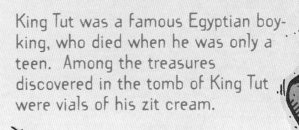

King Tut was a famous Egyptian boy-king, who died when he was only a teen. Among the treasures discovered in the tomb of King Tut were vials of his zit cream.

If the pore opens up and air reaches the junk inside, a blackhead forms. The back of a blackhead is not dirt. If you pinch a blackhead, the plug that comes out is old oil and skin pigment. The black plug will also just fall out on its own.

If the comedo doesn't open up, white blood cells collect in the area to eat up the material. Pus forms and moves to the surface. **A pimple is born.** The gross white tip of a zit squirts out if you squeeze it. The white stuff is mostly pus. If large amounts of pus build, a cyst forms.

Some people have oilier skin than other people. These people often develop more acne. Other people tell people they have acne because they eat chocolate or fried foods or because their hair hangs in their faces. These other people don't know what they are talking about. Neither food nor hair causes zits.

Y ou knew the cookie sheet was hot, but you just couldn't wait to grab a sugar-, oatmeal-, and flour-baked treat. Eeeeeowwwww! Your finger jerked away from the oven-heated metal faster than a jab delivered by a prize fighter. In seconds, your body goes into action to repair your damaged skin. Within several minutes, you notice the effort; a blister forms.

Blisters actually come in two varieties. Small blisters less than the size of a tackhead are called vesicles (VES eye culls). The word "vesicle" comes from a Latin word that means small bladder. If you've had chicken pox, you probably noticed many vesicles on your body. Chicken pox viruses, bug bites, drug reactions, and sunburn also form vesicles. Large blisters are called bullae (bee YOOL eee). This word is from the Latin word for bubble. Bullae pop up from burns, rubbing, and viruses that form cold sores. But no matter whether it is a vesicle or a bulla, it is still a blister. A blister is a blister is a blister.

The blister beetle is a type of beetle that was dried and powdered and used to raise blisters on a patient.

Blisters have this nasty habit of making us want to pop them. The little skin bump looks so much like a water balloon that you just can't help it. But your body does not make blisters to entertain you; it makes blisters to protect you. Your skin is like birthday cake because it too is made of layers. The top layer you see is the **epidermis (ep uh DUR miss).** *Epi* means outer, and *derm* is Greek for skin. The epidermis is actually layers of dead skin. Under the epidermis is the dermis. The dermis is alive with blood vessels, sweat glands, hair roots, and new skin cells. Skin cells are damaged from rubbing, which happens when you first walk in a new pair of shoes or when heat or a virus causes fluid from the blood to flow into the area. The liquid is mostly the fluid that blood cells float in mixed with the fluid that your body organs bathe in. Sometimes red blood cells also collect in the area, making an icky blood blister. The fluids pool between the dermis and the epidermis, and the top skin puffs up. If you press lightly on a blister, you can feel the body liquid inside.

The blister hangs around for a few days while your body repairs the skin. After the work is done, the blister bursts all by itself, or it dries up. Only, only, only if the blister is very, very, very painful should you break it with a sterilized needle. Otherwise, just cover it with a bandage so you won't even be tempted.

A blister infected with bacteria can get really gross. Lots of times a blister is doing fine all by itself, and then someone goes and bursts its bubble. Hundreds of bacteria that hang out on your skin rush in. The nice little bubble filled with clear fluid transforms into a yellowish, greenish pus-filled monster. The sound of the word "pus" tells you it is something putrid. Say it a few times: pus, pus, pus, pus. Even to pronounce the word, you curl up your lip and wrinkle your nose as if you are really disgusted.

Pus is pretty gross stuff. It's made of the clear, clean body fluids, a bunch of dead bacteria that were wiped out by your infection-fighting cells, and a bunch of dead fighting cells that were killed in the battle. All of the dead bacteria and cell bodies make the pus stink. A pus-filled blister is not a good blister. It may mean it's time to see a doctor.

Fake Blisters

What you need: Red food coloring, yellow food coloring, petroleum jelly, bowl, toothpick, a white tissue

What you do: Select a blister site. Place a dab of red food coloring onto the end of your finger, and smear an oval patch about the size of a mutated quarter at the blister site. Don't make the blister too big, or it won't look real. Place a fingerful of petroleum jelly into the bowl. Add a tiny drop of yellow food coloring and mix with the toothpick. Glob the yellowish petroleum jelly into the center of the red oval, molding it into a bubble shape. Separate the tissue into a single layer. Tear the tissue into an oval shape about the size of the red patch on your skin and lay the tissue over the blister glob. Gently smear clear petroleum jelly over the tissue until it becomes invisible. Clean up the edges and go show someone. Say, "Do you have a pitchfork, so I can pop this awful blister?"

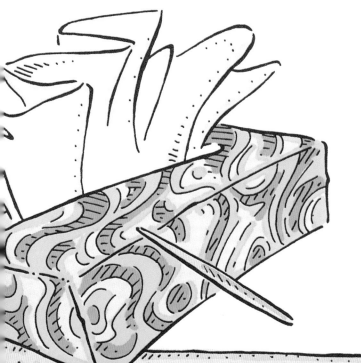

Dandruff

Any animal with hair, feathers, or skin has dandruff. Yes, that includes parakeets, kitties, and walruses. The only difference is that the flaky stuff is called dandruff on humans but dander on other animals.

Daily about ten billion tiny scales of skin rub off your body, float through the air and land on the floor, furniture, lawn, or other people. In a lifetime you could fill eight five-pound flour bags with dead skin. (Put that in your bread and eat it!) You see dead skin flakes each time you dust your dresser. Over three fourths of household dust is made of dead skin cells. New skin cells replace the ones you discard. Each fresh, outer skin layer will live for about twenty-eight days before it dies, dries, and drops off.

Usually people do not worry about the tiny bits of skin that continuously drop from their bodies until they see these flakes raining from their heads and onto their shoulders. They have dandruff! Some people become horrified by unsightly skin flakes. "Oh no! Other people can see my shedding skin. My life is ruined." They rush to the store, purchase shampoos and lotions, rub their scalps, and inspect their heads closely to make sure the nasty skin cells have at least disappeared from sight.

Dandruff does not cause baldness.

Dandruff is actually pretty normal. About half of all people between the ages of ten and twenty have dandruff. After age thirty, the numbers drop. Every three days your head makes a whole new set of skin cells. As with the rest of your body, dead cells on your head have to go somewhere, so they flake off. Unlike the rest of the dead skin cells on your body, however, the scalp cells become trapped in the hair. Oil from the glands in your head then collect on the skin cells stuck in hair prison. Dust and soot join the sticky, trapped skin cells. The combination of dead skin cells, oil, and dust forms greasy yellow or dry grayish white scales: dandruff. Most of the time the tiny flakes go down the drain when you wash your hair, but sometimes the flake factory or the oil makers go out of control to make visible dandruff.

Oil glands go cuckoo in teenagers. That's why dandruff, zits, and blackheads show up at about age twelve. Before this age, the joyous products of body oil are not very common. Teenagers and adults may also get dandruff from out-of-control skin shedding. No one really knows why this happens in some people. But it is certain that you cannot catch dandruff from a dandruffy brush or comb.

Newborn babies also get a type of dandruff called **cradle cap.** *But babies aren't teenagers!* Leftover chemicals from the mother's body cause the oil glands in the baby's head to become active after birth. Thanks, Mom. Baby dandruff is yellowish-brown, greasy, and crusty. "**Oh what a cute, little crusty head.**" Cradle cap only lasts a short while. Actually, the baby doesn't care because a baby doesn't even know what dandruff is.

Sometimes people totally panic when they have only fake dandruff. For instance, if you don't rinse all the shampoo out of your hair, the leftover soap will clump and chip off. It's not dandruff. **So rinse your hair really well.** A peeling sunburned head also looks like dandruff. **It is not dandruff; it is a peeling sunburn.** So wear a cap when you are out in the sun for long periods.

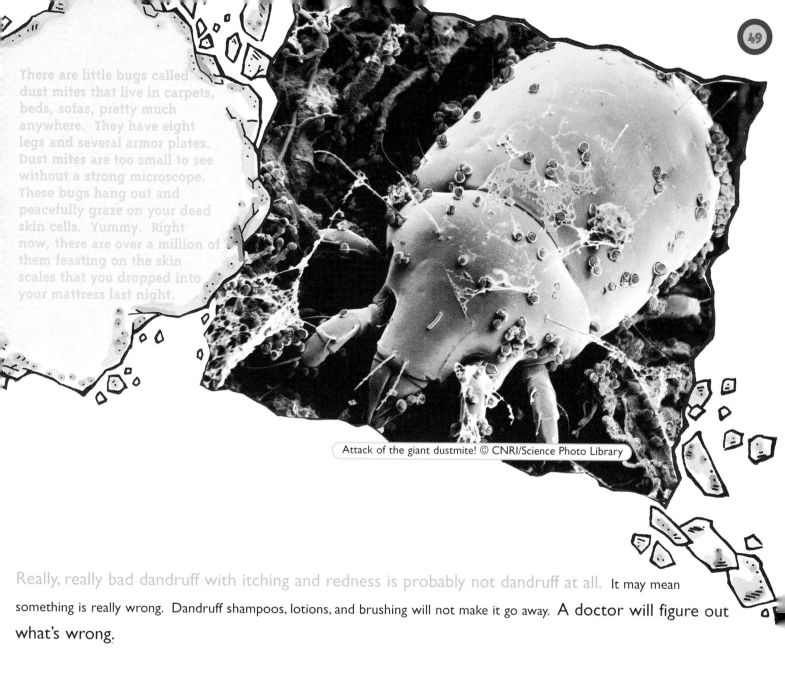

There are little bugs called dust mites that live in carpets, beds, sofas, pretty much anywhere. They have eight legs and several armor plates. Dust mites are too small to see without a strong microscope. These bugs hang out and peacefully graze on your dead skin cells. Yummy. Right now, there are over a million of them feasting on the skin scales that you dropped into your mattress last night.

Attack of the giant dustmite! © CNRI/Science Photo Library

Really, really bad dandruff with itching and redness is probably not dandruff at all. It may mean something is really wrong. Dandruff shampoos, lotions, and brushing will not make it go away. A doctor will figure out what's wrong.

So I know what dandruff is, but what should I do if I get it? OK, here are the dandruff basics: Don't panic. Wash your hair several times a week. Make sure you get all of the shampoo out of your hair. If a regular shampoo doesn't work, try a dandruff shampoo. Relax. Enjoy yourself. Dandruff doesn't harm anyone, even you.

Scabs and Wounds

Scabs and Wounds and Scabs Wounds and

It is one of the unanswered questions of the universe; why do people like to pick at scabs? Scabs are dried and clotted blood that serve as nature's bandage; they are not candy or luscious **treats.** A scab protects invaded and destroyed skin underneath until order is restored. The massacred area, or wound, is a miniature battleground. The body must protect itself from invading bacteria while it rebuilds the torn-up skin structure.

Your body has a built-in military, and a cut triggers a full attack. The cut allows enemy bacteria to invade. The bacteria flock to the area because blood is great for eating. The feasting bacteria, however, cause infection. So your body sounds the alarm. Chemicals attach to the invaders and send out homing information to the rest of the body's militia.

Also to the rescue is the fix-it crew. The first to arrive are tiny blood cells called **platelets** that barricade the area. Platelets usually flow along freely with the blood, but in the face of danger they change. The platelets become sticky. They clump together to form a plug that stops blood from leaking. That's why a small cut bleeds only for a couple of minutes.

Next the pooled blood in the wound begins to change. Ever touch a cut after a few minutes? The blood becomes jellylike, thick, and gooey. The goopy blood is a **clot**. The clot puts out threads that criss-cross to form a net. When the surface of the clot dries, it forms a delicious scab.

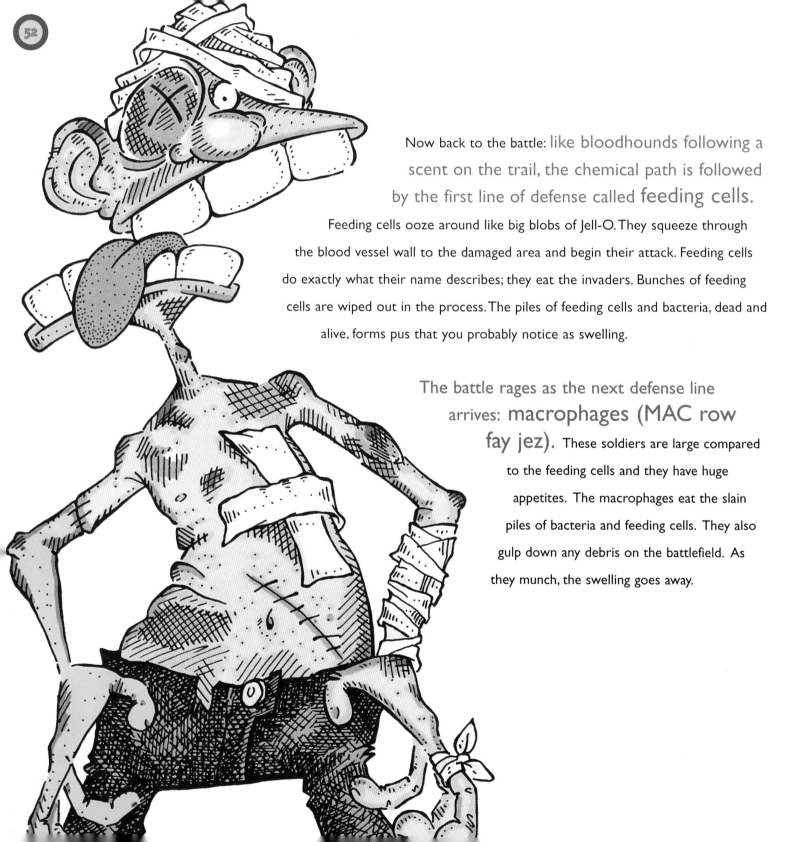

Now back to the battle: like bloodhounds following a scent on the trail, the chemical path is followed by the first line of defense called **feeding cells.**

Feeding cells ooze around like big blobs of Jell-O. They squeeze through the blood vessel wall to the damaged area and begin their attack. Feeding cells do exactly what their name describes; they eat the invaders. Bunches of feeding cells are wiped out in the process. The piles of feeding cells and bacteria, dead and alive, forms pus that you probably notice as swelling.

The battle rages as the next defense line arrives: **macrophages (MAC row fay jez).** These soldiers are large compared to the feeding cells and they have huge appetites. The macrophages eat the slain piles of bacteria and feeding cells. They also gulp down any debris on the battlefield. As they munch, the swelling goes away.

Although the major battle is over, the body releases one more line of defense. Behind the front line, these fighters search and destroy any bacteria that may have slipped away. The search and destroy cells are called killer cells, which seems like a pretty good name.

During the whole battle, the skin is being repaired. A thin layer of surface skin has formed below the scab. Special cells arrive under the scab and begin reconstruction. These cells make a tough material, called fibrin (FY brinn), that binds the gap together. After they are through, the scab falls off. Bon appétit.

The word scab comes from the Latin word *scabere* for "to scratch."

Fake Wounds

What you need: Petroleum jelly, red food coloring, petroleum jelly, four drops of red food coloring, bowl, a white tissue, powdered cocoa

What you do: In the bowl, place a fingerful of petroleum jelly, four drops of red food coloring, and a pinch of cocoa. Stir with the toothpick. Separate one layer from the tissue and rip out a small rectangle, about three inches by two inches. Place the tissue at your wound site and cover it with petroleum jelly. Now mold the goopy tissue to form a wound. The side of the wound should be higher than the center. Smear the blood-colored petroleum jelly in the center of the wound. Sprinkle cocoa onto the edges and rub the cocoa in to make the edges dark. You may want to add some cocoa to the center of the wound as well. Go show someone who gets really upset at the sight of blood or cuts; maybe they'll faint!

Eye gunk

You have seen these familiar scenes repeated in movies, commercials, and television. A young boy awakens and yawns. You see his eyes brighten. He rushes to the window to gaze at the beautiful snow or a bright summer day or the return of his long-lost dog. It is an OK scene, but something is missing. How about this one? A woman sleeps peacefully. She is awakened suddenly by a loud noise. A camera close-up shows terror in her eyes. Did you figure out the part that is absent? Here's one more. A man rolls over and hits the alarm clock. Suddenly his eyes pop open. He springs out of bed. He is in a big hurry, but he doesn't forget whatever the commercial is trying to sell. Give up yet? It's eye crust, or sleepies. None of the people on the screen ever wipes the gunk out of their eyes after they get up. Actually, they never even have eye crust to wipe away.

In real life, sleeping dust is just a regular part of the morning. You rub it away. It falls onto the floor or your bed. You don't really think too much about it. If you notice eye sand in someone else's eye, you try not to stare at it, or you tell the person to get rid of it. The odd thing about eye crust, sleep, sand man, sleeping dust, sleepie, eye gunk, or sleeper is that it has no common name. Yet it has been around for millions of years forming in human and animal eyes alike.

Eye gunk can be hard and crusty or gooey and stringy. It usually forms in the two places where the eyelids meet, the corners of your eye. Commissure (KOM a sure) is the scientific name for the spot where the eyelids join. Sometimes eye crust also forms along the lashes of your lower lid. In each commissure closest to your nose is a fleshy little bump. Go check it out in a mirror. Don't stick your finger in your eye.

Your tears are the best eyewash. But tired, itching eyes may sometimes need refreshing. Instead of buying eye drops from the drugstore, use a clean eyedropper and place one or two drops of cool tap water in your lower lids.

Just pull down your lower lid and inspect the bump. Then lift your upper lid and inspect the bump. This lump of flesh is called the caruncle (CAR ung cul). The caruncle is made of oil and sweat glands. The little glands squirt out the white goopy junk that sometimes collects in this corner of your eye. But sleepies and other types of eye gunk are more than the oozing from the caruncle.

Each eye has more than thirty glands that drip tear substances onto the eye. The names for some of the glands sound more like Greek gods than tear makers: the glands of Zeis, the glands of Krause, and the glands of Wolfring. The largest gland is almond shaped. It is located under your skin, above the outer corner of your eye between your upper lid and your eyebrow. Each year these glands squirt about eight pints of cleaning fluid, or tears, onto your eye. The tears flow across your eyeball, then drain through tiny holes in the commissure near your nose. The old tears flow into your nose, and you get rid of them by swallowing. So your nose is the dumping site for your tears, which explains why your nose runs when you cry.

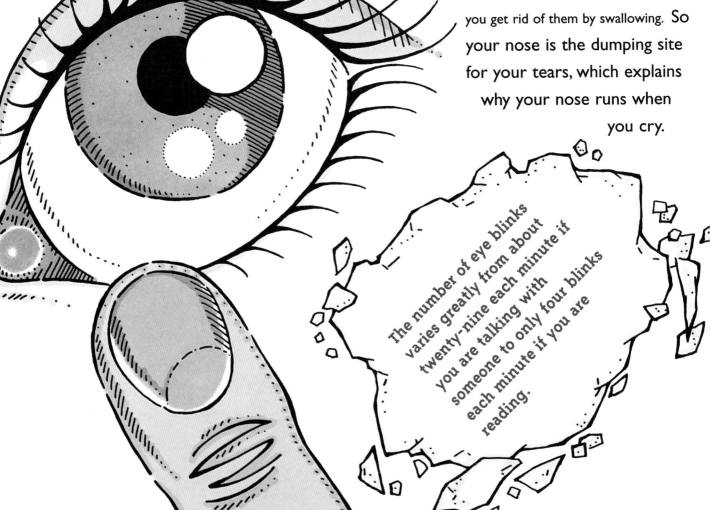

The number of eye blinks varies greatly from about twenty-nine each minute if you are talking with someone to only four blinks each minute if you are reading.

The tear film that bathes your eyeball has three layers. A mucus layer and an oily layer—made of wax, cholesterol (the same stuff you get in food), and other fats—sandwich the tear layer. The tear layer is a mixture of salts (which is why tears taste salty); sugar; ammonia (what you find in cleaning fluids); urea (which is also in pee); lots of water; the chemical in egg whites called albumin (al BEW min), citric acid like that in oranges and grapefruit; a chemical that destroys bacteria; and a few other things. *So what does all this tear stuff have to do with morning eye crust?*

Oh yes, back to eye crust: when you blink your eyes, your lids move tears across the surface of your eye. And you do this for one-fifth of a second twenty times each minute. You will actually spend five years of your life blinking. When your lids close during a blink, the little drain-holes close. *Eye crust, remember we were talking about eye crust.*

Now back to eye-crust formation: at night, you slam your eyelids shut to form a great waterproof seal. You make hardly any tears, but you do make some. The night tears seep along your eye and pool in the corners. Because the little drain-holes close when your lids snap shut, the tears don't drain away. The liquid in the tears evaporates to form little crusty masses. Mix these with a trace of sweat and oil from the caruncle and voilà—eye crust.

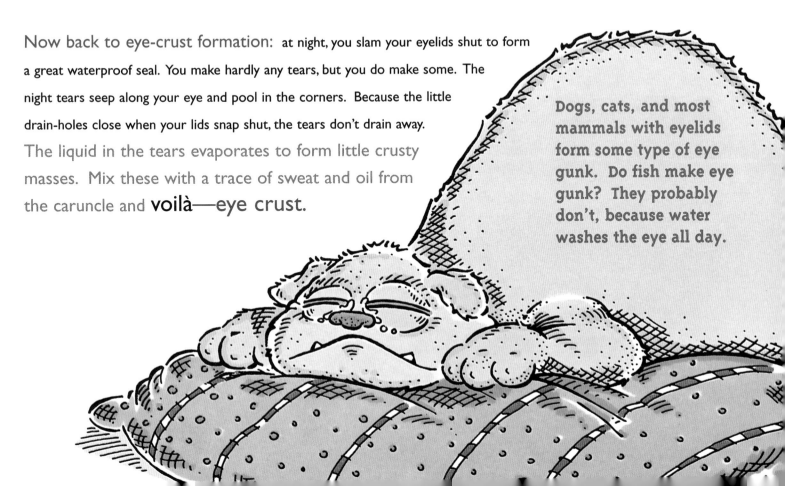

Dogs, cats, and most mammals with eyelids form some type of eye gunk. Do fish make eye gunk? They probably don't, because water washes the eye all day.

Tooth Tartar

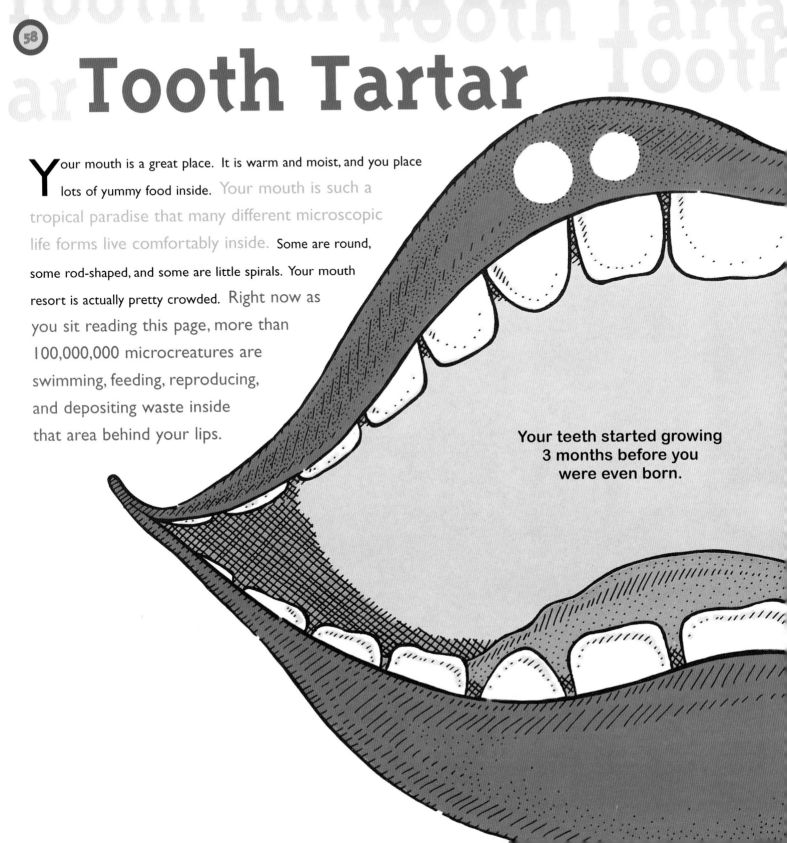

Your mouth is a great place. It is warm and moist, and you place lots of yummy food inside. Your mouth is such a tropical paradise that many different microscopic life forms live comfortably inside. Some are round, some rod-shaped, and some are little spirals. Your mouth resort is actually pretty crowded. Right now as you sit reading this page, more than 100,000,000 microcreatures are swimming, feeding, reproducing, and depositing waste inside that area behind your lips.

Your teeth started growing 3 months before you were even born.

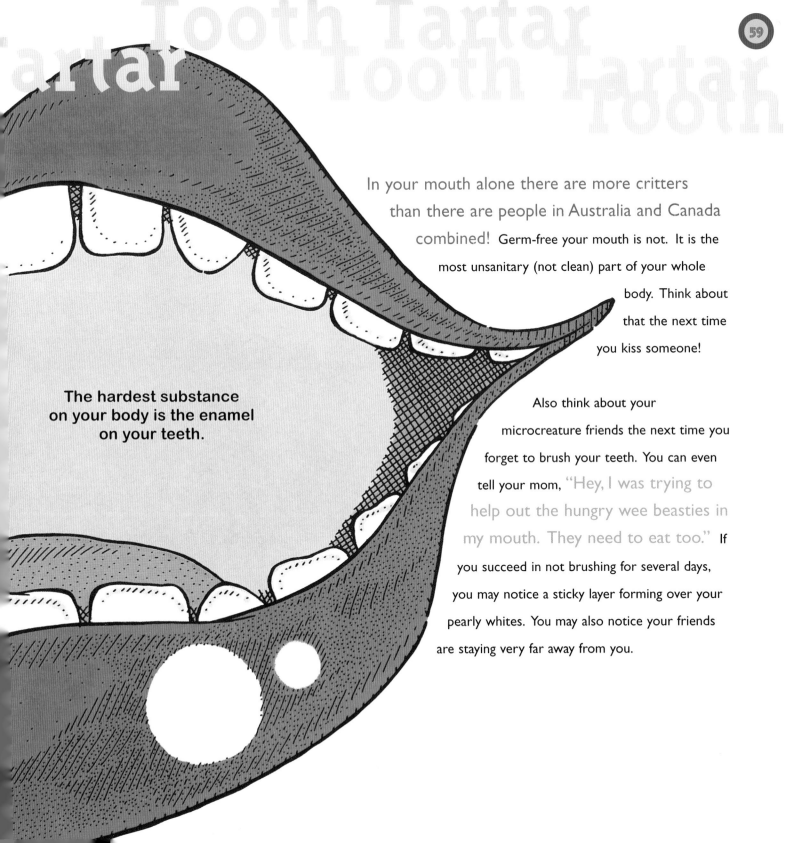

In your mouth alone there are more critters than there are people in Australia and Canada combined! Germ-free your mouth is not. It is the most unsanitary (not clean) part of your whole body. Think about that the next time you kiss someone!

Also think about your microcreature friends the next time you forget to brush your teeth. You can even tell your mom, "Hey, I was trying to help out the hungry wee beasties in my mouth. They need to eat too." If you succeed in not brushing for several days, you may notice a sticky layer forming over your pearly whites. You may also notice your friends are staying very far away from you.

The hardest substance on your body is the enamel on your teeth.

The scum layer you feel is called **plaque (plak)**. Plaque is a mixture of bits of leftover food, worn-out mouth cells, many bacteria, and bacteria waste. If you rub your tongue against your teeth, it feels pretty smooth, but your teeth really have tiny cracks and pits. The plaque collects in the cracks and pits as well as between the teeth. Plaque is invisible.

Inspect your teeth in the mirror, or inspect someone else's chompers. Look really closely where your teeth meet the gums. Did you notice yellowish or brownish stuff on some of the teeth? *Hey, wait. I thought plaque was invisible.* It is. The stuff you saw is many layers of hardened plaque called tartar, or scale. Tartar forms when minerals

This is a close-up photo of plaque—what you get when you don't brush your teeth! © David Scharf 1989

in saliva combine with slimy plaque and cement to your teeth. Scale builds up on your teeth stony layer by stony layer. People who don't brush their teeth a lot and don't use dental floss will have lots of scale.

So if you want lovely, yellow teeth, don't brush your teeth or floss and eat lots of candy, bread, and pasta.

Dentists remove tartar by scraping and chiseling it off the teeth. **Removing scale is called scaling.** The name isn't too original but I guess chipping, digging, and scraping rocky layers from teeth isn't too thrilling either. Ouch! Scrape! Ouch!

Plaque Check

In 1676, a Dutch drapery maker was the first person to discover bacteria. Antony van Leeuwenhoek made magnifying lenses as a hobby. One day he decided to look at plaque scrapings from his teeth. He was probably really surprised to find that tiny living things lived inside.

What you need: "Disclosing" tablets that you can buy at some drugstores or can get from your dentist, toothbrush, toothpaste, water

What you do: Brush your teeth normally; don't do the ultimate fantastic brush job that you do right before you go to the dentist. Put a disclosing tablet in your mouth. Chew, chew, chew the tablet. Use water to swish the tablet juices around in your smile. Look in the mirror and smile. Argh! What's wrong with my mouth? The disclosing tablets stuck to the plaque and dyed the places where you didn't brush. I hope you like having a colorful smile for awhile. No, just kidding. Brush your teeth to remove the plaque and the tablet stains from the spots that you missed.

Farts

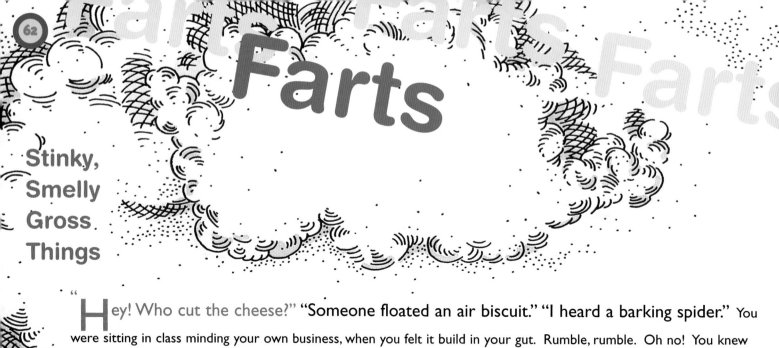

"**H**ey! Who cut the cheese?" "Someone floated an air biscuit." "I heard a barking spider." You were sitting in class minding your own business, when you felt it build in your gut. Rumble, rumble. Oh no! You knew what was to come. You squeezed tightly your anal exit. It was useless: the pressure and then the escape. Flub, flubba, fwwwp: you did it; **you farted.**

Medical people use the word **"flatus"** (FLATE us) for farts and **"flatulence"** (FLAT you lents) for farting. These words come from the Latin *flatus*, which means the act of blowing. That seems pretty accurate.

One scientist even did the stinky research to find out that a person farts about fourteen times every day. Some people putt more, and some even do it a lot. There was a man in Minneapolis, Minnesota, who kept a "flatographic" of his gas production. This guy had major gas. He

counted 141 farts in a twenty-four-hour period. Impressive! Keep count of your gas production. If you putt fourteen times in one day, you are pretty normal.

If you could capture the gases that exit your anal opening, you could measure them. This type of fart study has actually been conducted. According to an expert on gas passers, the amount of gas varies from one cup to one-half gallon per day.

Although you do it easily, making a fart is an involved process. After food is crushed in your stomach, it passes into the hose in your gut, or the small intestine. Here minerals, vitamins, and other important stuff moves through the walls of the small intestine into the blood. The mush then leaves the small intestine to enter the fart factory, the large intestine.

People Who Earn Money by Farting

The famous fart performer, Joseph Pujol, was a Frenchman who "outgrossed" the leading French stage artists of the mid 1800s. Pujol was known as "Le Pétomane," the fartomaniac. Pujol had the gift of being able to create different sounds of varying lengths from his orifice. At first he used his talent to amuse friends at parties. "Hey, let's invite Pujol. He's always a gas at parties." Once he matured, he took his act to the stage.

A current Japanese fartomaniac delivered a televised fart performance in 1980. The unidentified fartomaniac took the air waves and captivated audiences by farting over 3,000 times in a row, imitiating sounds with his anus, and playing songs from you know where. Now that's talent.

Some foods are still not broken down. These foods include wheat products, dairy products, cabbage, apples, radishes, broccoli, onions, cauliflower, and the magical food: beans. The undigested parts of these foods are fiber and some types of sugars. If you really want to toot, you should eat lots of food with fiber and indigestible sugar.

How to Say Fart in Various Languages

French	pet
Romanian	bah sheet
Vietnamese	dut
Czechoslovakian	purrrd note
Spanish	pay dough
Japanese	oh nowla
Gujarati Indian	pawd
German	furs
Mandarin China	fang pi
Taiwanese	bawng pwi
Tigrenya Eritrea	ki terret

Your large intestine is home to billions of tiny living creatures called bacteria. One type of bacteria in your large intestine is *E. coli*. The undigested food is dinner, lunch, or breakfast for the gut critters. The bacteria eat the fiber and other substances. Just as you produce waste after you eat, so do the bacteria. As the bacteria eat your unusable food, they fart inside you. Their gas builds in your intestine. When the pressure is too great, it exits through your butthole. So, you are just the storage container for the creatures that fart in you.

A fart is actually a mixture of gases. Most of it is carbon dioxide, hydrogen, and methane. These gases are odorless. Hydrogen gas is lighter than air, so it floats. Hydrogen and methane are highly flammable. Methane is used for stoves and gas heating. The smelly gases are indole (IN dohl), skatole (SCAT ohl), and hydrogen sulfide. Hydrogen sulfide makes the odor of rotten eggs. Indole and skatole perfume poop. (Your nose can detect a disgusting odor that has been diluted, or watered down, ten billion times.) Although the smelly gases are only a very small part of a fart, everyone knows when they escape.

Beside gas and odors, farts also make sounds. Think about the many fart sounds. Make a few of them with your mouth or by cupping your hand in your armpit and then flapping like a one-armed bird. There's the fwwt, the put-put-put, the pwwwbbbb, the flubba-flubb, and they're only a few of the many fart noises.

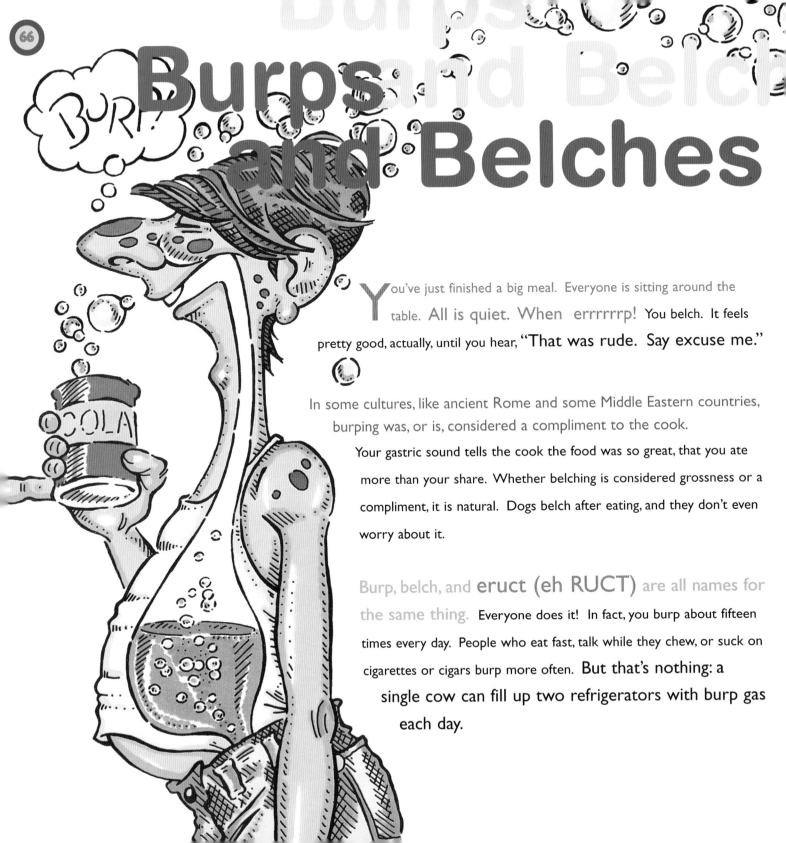

Burps and Belches

You've just finished a big meal. Everyone is sitting around the table. All is quiet. When errrrrrp! You belch. It feels pretty good, actually, until you hear, "That was rude. Say excuse me."

In some cultures, like ancient Rome and some Middle Eastern countries, burping was, or is, considered a compliment to the cook. Your gastric sound tells the cook the food was so great, that you ate more than your share. Whether belching is considered grossness or a compliment, it is natural. Dogs belch after eating, and they don't even worry about it.

Burp, belch, and **eruct (eh RUCT)** are all names for the same thing. Everyone does it! In fact, you burp about fifteen times every day. People who eat fast, talk while they chew, or suck on cigarettes or cigars burp more often. But that's nothing: a single cow can fill up two refrigerators with burp gas each day.

The burp source is your stomach. Your stomach is a small sac of muscles. Your stomach is connected on one end to your esophagus, which reaches up to your throat, and on the other end to your small intestine. There is always a little bit of air in the stomach. The stomach bubble is in the upper half of the stomach.

The stomach is like a balloon. The stomach stretches as food, liquid, and air are added. When you eat and drink, you swallow air, which adds gas to your stomach. When the stomach digests, it adds acid to the foods and creates gas of its own. So even more gas enters your stomach. If your stomach builds up too much gas, the pressure becomes too great. Gas must escape to release built-up pressure. Burp!

If you clamp your lips closed when you belch, you can burp through your nose. But is it still a burp?

Flavorful burps result from certain foods that you ingest into your stomach. The gases carry the odor along with the gas as it exits your mouth. Maybe you have shared the burpy air of a stranger and smelled garlic burps, onion burps, beer burps, vomit burps, or baloney burps. **Maybe you even tasted the smelly belches as you breathed in the stranger's belly air.** Yummy. It's so nice to share.

Belch Model

You will need: Vinegar, baking soda, medium or large balloon, funnel

What to do: If you do this over a sink, there is much less clean-up at the end. The balloon is your stomach. Pour a small amount of vinegar into the bottom of the balloon, your stomach. Use the funnel to add baking soda to the balloon stomach. Pinch the balloon closed with your fingers at the neck; this is your esophagus. Watch your balloon stomach expand with gas. Unpinch the esophagus to release the gas, or burp. Practice the pinch release to see whether you can make the belch model sound like a real burp.

B.O. and Sweat

When you get on the bus, does everyone, including the driver, get off? Does your family stay not only in a different room but also in a different house? Do dogs hang out with you more than humans do? **Maybe you have B.O.—body odor.** OK, maybe the description is exaggerated. But the American fear of body odor is not. Americans spend over 540,000,000 dollars each year trying to get rid of body odor.

Except for your lips and a couple of the reproductive parts, your body is covered with little sweat producers, or sweat glands. On your palm are more than 2,000 sweat glands in an area about the size of a postage stamp. Actually, the palms and the soles of your feet have more sweat glands than anywhere else on your body. And sweat glands ooze lots of sweat out of the little openings, or pores, in your skin. Up to a quart of liquid in an average day. *Hey, wait. People don't put deodorant on their palms, and I know the palms of my hands aren't stinky.* True, but there are two kinds of sweat, the not-so-stinky kind and the really smelly kind.

Looking for a new career? How about deodorant tester? © Louis Psihoyas Matrix

Smelly sweat comes from sweat glands located mostly in the armpits but also in the crotch, anus, and a little on the scalp. Until a person gets to be about twelve years old, these glands don't do anything. After age twelve or so, they start oozing, and they never stop. That's why adults are so stinky, and kids aren't. Grown-up sweat is a sticky, milky, gluey liquid that dribbles in little beads from the pores. The balls of sweat smell a little like the cleaning fluid called ammonia, but it's pretty much odorless. *Hey, wait again. I wouldn't go around sniffing people's armpits. Everyone knows that underarms smell putrid and disgusting.* Right again. The sticky sweat doesn't smell until bacteria munch on it. Unlike the not-so-stinky sweat, smelly sweat has stuff in it that bacteria like to eat. The fuzzy, round armpit bacteria change the sweat to make it stinky.

Dogs don't have many sweat glands, so they sweat by panting. A cat's sweat glands are in the soft pads on the bottom of the feet.

That's where a "reverse the odor," or a deodorant, comes in handy. To get rid of the smell, deodorants contain chemicals that poison the stink-making bacteria. A smear of the poison wipes out most of the critters clinging to the armpit hairs or hanging out on the surface of the skin. Some of the bacteria do escape the attack by hiding at the base of the hairs or by falling from the armpit to rest on another part of the body. After the slaughter, these bacteria return to the armpit home to begin munching and reproducing, until the next deodorant attack or soap-and-water cleaning.

During the Middle Ages, bathing was not in style. Not having to bathe was a sign of wealth. Many rich people bragged about avoiding bath water. One Englishman did not take the plunge for thirteen years. Not bathing, however, meant that people did sweat and stink. People covered up their stench with perfumes, oils, and spices. A stinky time was had by all.

Odor-producing bacteria don't like to eat the other kind of sweat very much. The sweat that squirts from millions of other pores on your body is actually very weak urine (yes, urine) with some other stuff thrown in. Just like pee, sweat is a combination of water, salts, and urea (yur EE a). It also contains a chemical that is the same as wasp poison and another chemical similar to the stuff that skunks spray.

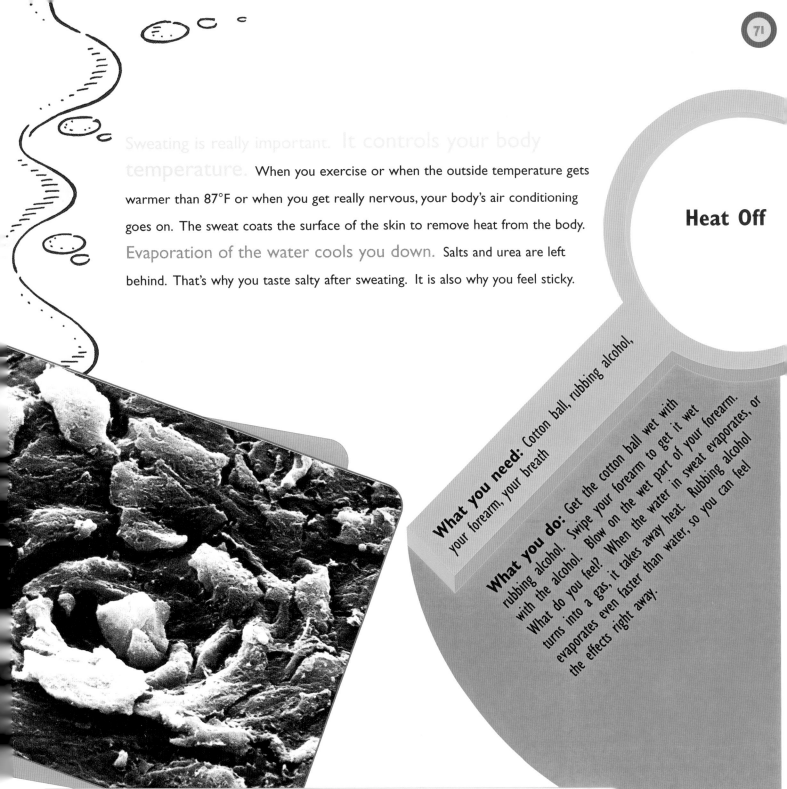

Heat Off

Sweating is really important. It controls your body temperature. When you exercise or when the outside temperature gets warmer than 87°F or when you get really nervous, your body's air conditioning goes on. The sweat coats the surface of the skin to remove heat from the body. Evaporation of the water cools you down. Salts and urea are left behind. That's why you taste salty after sweating. It is also why you feel sticky.

What you need: Cotton ball, rubbing alcohol, your forearm, your breath

What you do: Get the cotton ball wet with rubbing alcohol. Swipe your forearm to get it wet with the alcohol. Blow on the wet part of your forearm. What do you feel? When the water in sweat evaporates, or turns into a gas, it takes away heat. Rubbing alcohol evaporates even faster than water, so you can feel the effects right away.

Is it a volcano? Nope. It's an opening for a sweat gland on someone's thumb. © Dr. Tony Brain/Science Photo Library

Bad Breath

Bad Breath Bad Breath Bad

"OK. 1 . . . 2 . . . 3 . . . . Take a deep breath. Hold. Release." You probably take a breath about twelve times each minute. If you have a calculator handy, you can figure out how many breaths you take in a year, in a lifetime. And each breath takes in about one-half liter (a little over one-half quart) of air. The same amount of gas moves out after it passes through your lungs.

Everyone around you takes hundreds of breaths each day. Most of the time people do so without anyone noticing, until someone near you has bad breath. Then each breath, every word (*don't even mention a cough*) is a foul reminder that you share the air with those around you. For your survival, you could offer the owner of the sour mouth a breath mint or maybe a whole pack of breath mints.

Almost everyone occasionally has bad breath. *Moi? No!* If you don't think that you do, imagine how your mouth tastes right after you wake up each morning. The comforting part is that brown mouth, or morning breath, is a temporary condition. Read the section on tooth tartar. There you learn that

a huge population of wee critters called **bacteria live in your mouth.** During the day, you swallow, talk, and drink liquids that wash the beasties and food particles down your throat into your stomach. When you sleep, your mouth stays quiet. The bacteria feast on the food particles and leave behind wastes during the night. When you wake up, you taste and smell the results of the bacteria party in your mouth. Each morning, many people run tight lipped to the bathroom to gargle before opening their mouths to say **"good morning."** Although mouthwash does remove most of the bacteria, the whole population returns within a couple of hours. Brushing your teeth is the best trick for combating morning mouth.

The scientific word for "swallowing" is "deglutition." Geez, it seems a lot easier to just say "swallow!"

"Onions, onions, ha, ha, ha," and garlic also produce interesting breath. Again, running to the medicine cabinet to gargle is fruitless. Onion and garlic breath does not even come from the mouth, but from the lungs. *Right, I know that a spaghetti dinner ends up in my stomach and not in my lungs.* From your stomach the food goes into your intestines, or guts. Most substances pass through the walls of the intestines into your blood. The smelly part of onions and garlic get into your blood that way. When the onion- or garlic-perfumed blood reaches your lungs, you breathe out flavored gas. The only solutions are not to eat garlic and onions or to take breath mints or just to wait it out surrounded by a group of people who ate the same dinner.

Smokers always have bad breath because the smoke contaminates the lungs. Even when they are not smoking, a clean air breath picks up some of the junk left behind in the lungs. The polluted air is released to give smokers a very a . . . a . . . distinct breath.

During normal breathing, the speed that you exhale air is about four miles per hour. During a sneeze, the air speed can reach up to forty miles per hour.

Continuous bad breath or chronic halitosis (hal uh TOE sis) is an odor of another kind. A person with halitosis could eat a ton of breath mints, gargle gallons of mouthwash, brush a hundred times a day, never eat onions, and still have bad breath. Sinus infections, allergies, decaying teeth, diseased gums, and digestive problems are just a few of the reasons for constant gross breath. Mouthwash is not the cure. Seeing a dentist or a doctor should help.

A giant fear of the bad-breath monster worries far too many people needlessly. Just relax, brush your teeth, and ask a close friend to tell you if your mouth smells like an outhouse.

Every Breath You Take

What you need: A calculator

What you do: You breathe twelve times each minute. To find out how many times you breathe in one hour, multiply 12 by 60. For the number of breaths in one day, multiply your answer by 24. Now take this answer and multiply it by 365 to find out how many times you breathe in one year. To calculate the number of breaths you have taken in your life, multiply the breaths in one year by your age. For figuring out how much air this is, choose an amount and multiply by 0.5 or one-half. By using the proper answers from your calculations, you can tell how many liters of air you expel each minute, hour, day, year, or lifetime. The next time you are in the soda section of the grocery store, count how many liters you breathe in one hour.

Smelly Feet

Maybe you know people who could knock you over just by taking off their shoes. Actually, no one has feet that smell like roses. We all have stinky feet at one time or another, and placing the blame on your tootsies isn't fair. Think about it—dogs, cats, rabbits, guinea pigs, and canaries don't have smelly feet. **If humans wore only sandals or no shoes at all, our feet would not smell either.** The real stench culprit is shoes and socks.

Feet sweat. Feet sweat a lot. About 250,000 little holes, or pores, on the soles of your feet squirt one-quarter cup of sweat each day. The palms of your hands are the only other place on your body that have so many sweat glands. Yet your hands don't stink. The sweat on your palms is allowed to evaporate into the air.

Odds are one of your feet is bigger than the other.

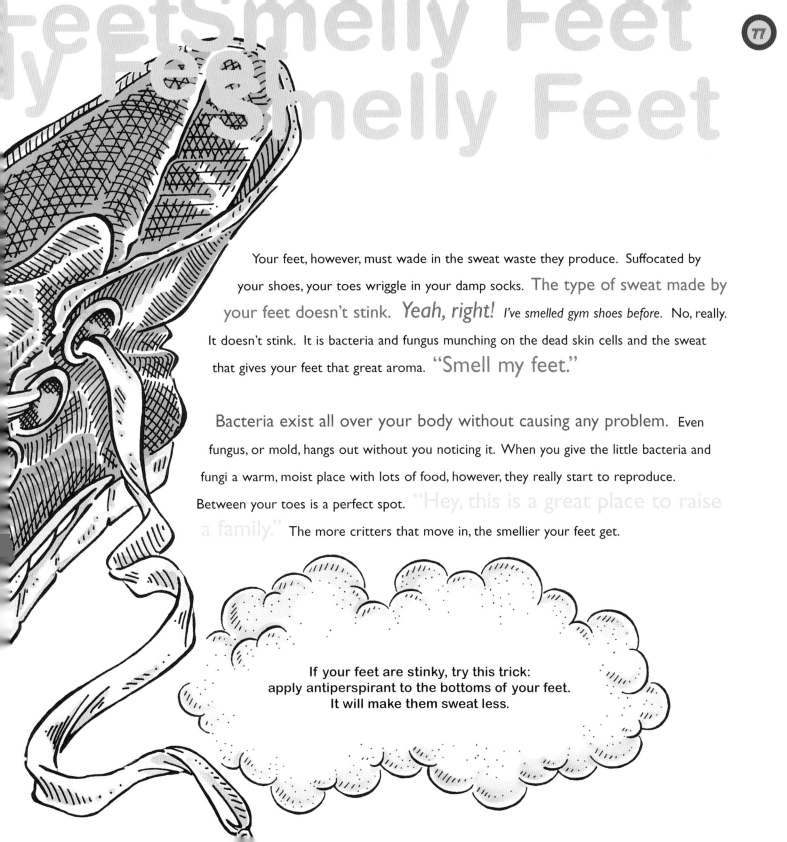

Your feet, however, must wade in the sweat waste they produce. Suffocated by your shoes, your toes wriggle in your damp socks. The type of sweat made by your feet doesn't stink. *Yeah, right!* *I've smelled gym shoes before.* No, really. It doesn't stink. It is bacteria and fungus munching on the dead skin cells and the sweat that gives your feet that great aroma. "Smell my feet."

Bacteria exist all over your body without causing any problem. Even fungus, or mold, hangs out without you noticing it. When you give the little bacteria and fungi a warm, moist place with lots of food, however, they really start to reproduce. Between your toes is a perfect spot. "Hey, this is a great place to raise a family." The more critters that move in, the smellier your feet get.

If your feet are stinky, try this trick:
apply antiperspirant to the bottoms of your feet.
It will make them sweat less.

The medical term for foul foot odor is **bromidrosis (bro mih DRO sis).** The "brom" part of the word comes from the Greek word for bad smell. The treatment of bromidrosis is pretty simple. Wash your feet each day; dry them well, especially between the little piggies; then sprinkle them with

The National Rotten Sneaker Championship takes place in Montpelier, Vermont. People show up wearing dirty, old, and very, very, very stinky sneakers. The contest winners get a new pair of sneakers and a can of foot powder.

foot powder. Wear shoes that allow your feet to breathe. Rubber, plastic, or vinyl shoes are perfect choices if you want foot odor. Do not wear the same socks or the same shoes every day. Also don't forget to wash your socks and your tennis shoes. Finally, take off your shoes and let your feet breathe. AHHHH Fresh air.

For some poor tootsies the smelly factor is so great that they need to be treated by a foot doctor, or podiatrist (poh DIE a trist). Maybe it is the foot doctor and not the feet that we should feel sorry for. The doctor has patients soak their feet in a solution as electricity is zapped through. Sounds pleasant.

There once was a man on the telly,
Whose feet they were so very smelly,
When he took off his shoes,
His friends said, "Peeee U."
You can smell them clear out to New Delhi!

The man had to find a solution,
To the source of his strong air pollution.
So he cut off his feet
And he buried them deep.
The dirt made for good stench dilution.

The lesson of this one is quick.
If the smell of your feet makes you sick,
Wash and powder each day
And the stench goes away
And your feet will always smell slick.

Hey, Good News! More GROSSOLOGY® Books!

Wow! Don't miss these other incredibly disgusting Grossology titles! (They should be available at whatever bookstore you like to visit. If not, the bookstore can always order them for you. Enjoy!)

GROSSOLOGY AND YOU

Picking up where *Grossology* left off, this further exploration of your body's most icky characteristics includes everything from goosebumps to hiccups, constipation to knuckle cracking, and rashes to warts—all explained in kid-friendly, scientifically correct terms.

ANIMAL GROSSOLOGY

Just when you thought it was safe, Grossology is back with a look at the most repulsive habits of our animal friends. You'll learn about slimy creatures, vomit munchers, blood suckers, and unforgettable animal poops.

GROSSOLOGY BEGINS AT HOME

Yup, there's a whole world of grossness right under your nose. Or behind your bed. Or between your toes. Or. . . you get the idea. Your home is the perfect laboratory for the science of really putrid things. So take a tour of your very own little house of yuckiness with Grossology as your guide.